Francis E. Clark

Fellow Travellers

A Personally Conducted Journey in Three Continents, with Impressions of Men,

Things and Events

Francis E. Clark

Fellow Travellers

A Personally Conducted Journey in Three Continents, with Impressions of Men, Things and Events

ISBN/EAN: 9783337128043

Printed in Europe, USA, Canada, Australia, Japan

Cover: Foto ©Andreas Hilbeck / pixelio.de

More available books at **www.hansebooks.com**

THE TAJ MAHAL

Fellow Travellers

A Personally Conducted Journey in Three Continents, with Impressions of Men, Things and Events

BY

Rev. Francis E. Clark, D.D.

President of the World's Christian Endeavor Union

New York   Chicago   Toronto
Fleming H. Revell Company
M DCCC XCVIII

Copyright, 1898
BY
FLEMING H. REVELL COMPANY

To My Dear Friends and Co-workers

JOHN WILLIS BAER

WILLIAM SHAW

AND

AMOS R. WELLS

WHOSE FAITHFULNESS, EARNESTNESS AND WISDOM IN
CHRISTIAN ENDEAVOR AT HOME,
MADE POSSIBLE MY JOURNEY FOR CHRISTIAN
ENDEAVOR IN LANDS AFAR,
THIS VOLUME IS AFFECTIONATELY

DEDICATED.

Contents

CHAPTER		PAGE
	By Way of Introduction	9
I.	The Battle of the Clouds	13
II.	Concerning Moral Mountain-Climbing	20
III.	The Land of William Tell	24
IV.	A Lesson from the Jungfrau	30
V.	Christian Endeavor in Switzerland	34
VI.	Good News Concerning Kristna Endeavourföreningarnas	38
VII.	Concerning Much Wandering in Many Lands	42
VIII.	Frederick Brotherton Meyer	46
IX.	The Ploughman Poet—1796–1896	53
X.	Three Thousand Miles in Germany	60
XI.	Two Famous Germans in the Class-room	65
XII.	Some Things in Germany Worth Copying	73
XIII.	Naples by Night	78
XIV.	The Oldest and the Youngest; or, Christian Endeavor in the Land of the Pyramids	85
XV.	A University Where "The Sun Do Move"	89
XVI.	Concerning Many Things on Sea and Shore	96
XVII.	A Plague-Stricken City	100
XVIII.	Concerning a Delightful Experience	115
XIX.	A Queer Hospital	120
XX.	Here and There in India	127
XXI.	Christian Endeavor in Historic India	132

Contents

CHAPTER		PAGE
XXII.	A Christian Endeavor Meeting in the Taj Mahal	137
XXIII.	Christian Endeavor on the Ganges	144
XXIV.	An Hour on the Ganges . . .	148
XXV.	The Famine at Short Range . .	154
XXVI.	Rocked on the Bosom of the Ganges	161
XXVII.	A Missionary Mecca	166
XXVIII.	Concerning a Unique and Memorable Convention	171
XXIX.	The Song of the Murderer of Thirty	179
XXX.	A Long Forward Step	185
XXXI.	In the Southern Empire . . .	189
XXXII.	Swami Vivekananda upon His Native Heath.	194
XXXIII.	Our Sixty Days in India . . .	199
XXXIV.	A Sky Pilot on a Coolie Ship . .	205
XXXV.	Twenty-three Days at Sea and Some Reflections	212
XXXVI.	Africa at Last	217
XXXVII.	The African at Home	222
XXXVIII.	The Two Republics of the Southern Cross	229
XXXIX.	A Call on "Oom Paul"	244
XL.	In the Orange Free State . . .	251
XLI.	How Bishop Taylor Read the Bible	255
XLII.	The World's Great Diamond Vault	261
XLIII.	Unto the Third and Fourth Generation	272
XLIV.	Last Days in South Africa . . .	284

List of Illustrations

THE TAJ MAHAL	*Frontispiece*
ON THE RIFFELBERG	*Facing page* 16
A SHEIKH OF THE DESERT	" " 86
A BURNING GHAT	" " 98
MARBLE SCREEN IN PALACE IN DELHI	" " 132
SOME OF DR. CLARK'S SNAP-SHOTS	" " 162
A SCENE IN INDIA	" " 190
AN AFRICAN KRAAL	" " 223
RUNAWAY KRAAL GIRLS IN A MISSION SCHOOL	" " 252

By Way of Introduction

This book is a transcript of actual travels, and was written, for the most part, on a steamer's deck, in the sleeping cars of India, and in a compartment of a South African train. It was written to real people; not to a possible and imaginary audience, but to people whom I knew and loved, who represented a great many more whom I did not know. I tried, so far as possible, to see what my friends would best like to see, and to keep my ears open to what they would best like to hear. In fact, the book is what its title claims, a personally conducted journey for all who care to read it.

This accounts for its structure and characteristics. It does not pretend exhaustively to "do" any one country. The things that interested me most in each country, I have tried to describe as best I could. I have no apology to make for the lack of a connected narrative, or for describing in one section a bit of enchanting scenery, in another, an eminent man whom I met, and in the next, a Christian Endeavor convention that had some striking and unusual points of interest. The book was meant to be of this character, and was intended to describe only the scenes and persons and events that interested the author at the time.

There is no lack of orderly and exhaustive books of travel. I myself have been guilty of adding one or two to the long list. But there is also room, I believe, for a book of this description, where orderliness of arrangement is sacrificed to what the author believes to be of most interest to his readers, and geography figures less than men and women and events.

As the long journey of nearly forty thousand miles here described, occupying almost a year, was undertaken solely for the advancement of the Christian Endeavor cause, the time was largely spent in attending conventions. I have not described many of these in detail, because, though most of them were extremely interesting and inspiring, they were necessarily of a somewhat local character. Still, not a few of the chapters relate to matters of special interest to Christian Endeavorers. If these frequent meetings, with their attendant duties, prevented in many cases much sight-seeing, this lack was made up by the more intimate glimpses of life in unusual conditions which the mere sight-seer could not have obtained, for the distinctive purpose of my journey opened many doors that would otherwise have been closed. Through these doors I will attempt to take my readers.

My hearty acknowledgments are due the

By Way of Introduction

Christian Endeavor World, in which many of these chapters originally appeared, the *North American Review,* the *American Review of Reviews,* Lippincott's *Magazine,* the *Temple Magazine* of London, the New York *Independent,* the *Sunday School Times,* the *Congregationalist,* and *Christian Work,* for permission to use in book form articles which were printed in their pages.

Fellow Travellers

I

THE BATTLE OF THE CLOUDS

My first chapter shall not describe the oft-related journey across the seas, the embarkation or the landing of the voyagers bound on this new pilgrimage, neither will it describe certain Christian Endeavor meetings and greetings in Paris and elsewhere that occupied the beginning of the journey; but it will take my readers directly to the heart of Switzerland, where we will enjoy a bit of Alpine scenery and a breath of vacation ozone, before undertaking the more serious purposes and duties that await us further on.

One of our memorable experiences was on the Riffelberg in a tempest. Let me attempt to describe it.

Who has not laughed over Mark Twain's exceedingly funny take-off of the dilettante Swiss tourists who climb the Alps (all that can be climbed by the funicular and rack-and-pinion railways) with tall silk hats, dress suits, and Saratoga trunks?

You remember he started up the Riffelberg, resolved to do or die, with a huge retinue, in which were sixteen barkeepers, two Latinists, and one chaplain, if I remember correctly.

The expedition got lost, and a long rope was tied to one of the guides, who was sent off to find the path. But he got tired of his job, hitched the rope to a ram, and went back to Zermatt. Various other adventures befell this expedition, all told in Mark's inimitable way.

But the Riffelberg has been able to stand all this ridicule. It does not hide its undiminished head, except occasionally behind a bank of clouds; and every year it attracts increasing crowds of tourists, two-thirds of whom, at least, I suppose, chuckle in half a dozen different languages (if it is possible to chuckle in different languages) over the humorist's chaff, as they go puffing up the pine-clad hill, on which it would be about as easy to get lost as for a farmer's boy to lose himself in going from the back door to the old well-sweep behind the barn.

One day in the holiday season, three Americans might have been seen about eight o'clock in the morning, starting out from Zermatt, with stout alpenstocks and their inevitable Baedeker. They had been anxiously scanning the clouds and studying the mercury, and, though both insisted on going down, the one over the highest mountain-peaks, and the other below " Variable" in the barometer tube, they determined to start.

The Matterhorn, to be sure, persistently kept on his cap of clouds; most impolitely, considering the many tourists that had come to do him reverence that day. Monte Rosa was tipped with a cloud fleck, too, or rather, wore around her neck a gauzy scarf, such as, I believe, ladies used very appropriately to call a "cloud," while her silvery head peered out above, radiant in the sunlight. This was discouraging, but the Breithorn shone resplendent without a cloud on her vast white bosom; the Weisshorn, too, was visible from head to heels; Castor and Pollux, like two gigantic good-natured twins (each rising to an altitude of about thirteen thousand feet), beckoned us on; mighty Lysskamm promised a good day; and so we started.

In spite of Mark Twain's chaff, the Riffelalp is a very respectable hill, even for Switzerland. Up, up, we climbed, the zigzags ever growing steeper and stonier, and the views ever more magnificent as each turn revealed some new glory. But always the Lion of Zermatt, the mighty Matterhorn, was in our eye. We could not get away from it. Turn which way we would, it seemed to dominate the landscape. Like a mighty cathedral tower, fifteen thousand feet high, built by God of solid rock, we could seem to feel its presence, even when we did not actually see it; and the higher we won our way up the Riffelberg, the more stupendous and majestic grew that mighty mass of rock and snow.

We made our way past the old church where are buried two of the rash climbers who first tried in 1865 to learn the secrets of the Matterhorn, over the bridge that spans the roaring Visp just set free from the icy fetters of the glacier, through the woods of spruce and hard pine, until, after two hours of tolerably hard climbing, we came to the Riffelalp hotel, one of the splendid hostelries that the canny Swiss have planted on every coign of vantage in their picturesque domain.

We press on more rapidly, for the clouds are coming down lower and lower on Mount Cervin, as the French call the Matterhorn. Not only his head, but his shoulders, his trunk, his hips, are covered now. Even the lower peaks put on their hoods; the wind rises and howls around our defenceless heads, as if it would blow us from the insecure ledge of rock around which we are trying to make our way, for we are far above the tree-line now. The rain begins to patter down; and, as we get higher, it turns to pellets of hail, which cut our faces and hands like minute bullets shot from an invisible catapult. But here we are at last, just as the storm begins in good earnest, at the Riffelhaus,

ON THE RIFFELBERG

another famous hotel, and one of the highest in all the Alps. Most grateful, too, is the warm fire and good cheer within.

From behind the ample vestibule, screened by glass on all sides, we watch the gathering tempest. Great, billowy masses of storm-laden clouds sweep up from the Zermatt valley on the one side, and from the Zmutt valley on the other, while down from every titanic mountain peak other battalions of clouds rush to meet them. The Matterhorn wholly disappears from view; Monte Rosa vanishes behind her veil; even white breasted Breithorn, nearest of all, is suddenly blotted out, as if it had never existed. All the world is without form and void. Chaos reigns supreme.

Louder and louder the demons of the air howl and shriek around us, but we can laugh at them behind the thick walls of our stone fortress. They cannot make it quiver. The rains descend and the floods come, and they beat upon that house; but it falls not. Then the snow drives down from the top of the highest Alps, where it has its perpetual home. A whitish tinge is given to the sombre cloud, and unfortunate tourists, who had set out for distant peaks before the storm arose, begin to straggle into the hotel by twos and threes, their faces reddened and parboiled by the snowy blast, and their black coats covered with nature's ermine.

Thus for four hours the storm rages, each moment more furious, and the cloud in which we are wrapped grows denser and blacker; when, look! look! by some invisible hand, in a single instant of time, quicker than on a mimic stage a curtain could be lifted, the cloud curtain is rolled away, and in majestic splendor the Matterhorn and all his magnificent brethren of Valais shine out flawless, speckless, immaculately grand. Below surge the baffled clouds, which the north wind is driving before him, filling the valleys, piling thick and deep upon the Görner Glacier below.

At once we start for the Görner Grat, a rocky, snow-bound peak two hours' climb above the Riffelberg, a peak more than ten thousand feet above the sea. A little one, indeed, is the Görner Grat among the thousands of Switzerland, but it lifts its modest head in the very centre of the mightiest mountains of Europe, and looks them all in the eye.

As we climb the snowy, toilsome steep, we witness many a battle between the north wind and the sulky clouds, which refuse to give up, beaten. Every few minutes they return to the attack, and apparently sweep all before them. One minute, we are standing in brilliant sunlight; the next, in impenetrable fog so dense and dark that we almost fear we shall lose the path. Then the next moment the north wind "cometh and cleanseth them," and all is sweet and clear again.

Perhaps the most beautiful sight of all was when the wind began to gain the mastery, and the highest peaks, crowned with sunlight, would peer above the clouds, enormously exaggerated, and looking fifty thousand, instead of fifteen thousand, feet high, seeming to hang and topple over us, almost from the zenith itself.

But old Boreas wins the day in the end; gloomily and sulkily the clouds retire; and, by the time we reach the top of the Görner Grat, every glorious peak in the magnificent circle, from the knife-edge of the Matterhorn's summit, clear around the horizon to the Matterhorn again, stands out sharp and brilliant as when first from the chisel of the great Sculptor. It was a magnificent battle, and we are thankful that it was our good fortune to witness it.

II

CONCERNING MORAL MOUNTAIN-CLIMBING

LET me take a text from the great mountains that, as I write, hem me in on every side. Before me, as I look out of the window in Montreux, are the rugged, ragged peaks of the Savoy Alps; behind loom up the Rochers de Naye and symmetrical Jaman, while off to the right, his head buried in the clouds, are the vast, snowy shoulders of the Dent du Midi.

But, like a good many other preachers, I am going to leave my text as soon as I can, taking it, as the fashion often is, for a point of departure alone. While these giant mountain peaks are beautiful to look upon, and magnificently imposing in their proportions, they are far from desirable places to make one's home, and I would rather end my life amid the lesser glories and tamer scenery of Oshkosh or Kalamazoo or Auburndale than amid these snow-clad, lofty heights.

So I think it is—to leave my text and get down to my homily—with our every-day lives. A great deal more depends upon what we deem dull, commonplace, and prosaic than upon the occasional lofty mountains of achievement. In fact, I doubt whether in the moral world there are any startling Alpine heights to be climbed in a single journey. Our daily ascent is more like our journey across the Nebraska prairies and the Colorado plains from the Missouri River to the Rocky Mountains. We are going up hill all the way, but so gradually that we do not know it until at last we stand five thousand feet above the sea, under the very shadow of Pike's Peak itself.

So every duty done, every act of kindness rendered, takes us one step up the hill, an inappreciable step, perhaps, a monotonous, weary sort of a step oftentimes, but yet a step that leads to real heights of moral grandeur.

I was especially impressed with this thought recently while reading a book of Robert Louis Stevenson's entitled "Across the Plains." It is a description, in his own inimitable style, of a journey taken in an emigrant train across America to the Pacific coast in the early days of his poverty and obscurity. In those days (it was nearly thirty years ago) the horrors of an uncomfortable, hard-seated, ill-smelling emigrant train to a sick and sensitive man must have been almost unendurable. I am sorry to find that he remarks more than once, for I fear there is more truth in it than we could wish, "Civility is the main comfort you miss in America." But among all the boorish passengers and snappish conductors and rude brakemen he found one newsboy who sweetened and lightened the journey by innumerable little acts of kindness. This is the way in which he has immortalized the cheery face and kindly deeds of that unknown newsboy :—

The lad who rode with us in this capacity from Ogden to Sacramento made himself the friend of all, and helped us with attention, assistance, and a kind countenance. He told us when and where we should have our meals and how long the train would stop, kept seats at table for those who were delayed, and watched that we should neither be left behind nor unduly hurried. You who live at ease at home can hardly realize the greatness of this service, even had it stood alone. When I think of that lad coming and going, train after train, with his bright face and civil words, I see how easily a good man may become a benefactor of his kind. Perhaps he is discontented with himself, perhaps troubled with ambition. Why, if he but knew it, he is a hero of the old Greek stamp; and, while he thinks he is only earning a profit of a few cents, he is doing a man's work and bettering the world.

In a Christian Endeavor meeting in Paris, the testimony that touched my heart the most was that of a young lady, who told us how, when she first spoke for her Master in an Endeavor meeting, hesitating and trembling and afraid of her own voice, as she sat down, a little girl by her side, who knew of her bashfulness, reached over and took her hand with a comforting squeeze. She said no word, but that gesture told of the little girl's love and sympathy. It was one of the steps that unconsciously led two souls up the table-lands and into the sunlight of God's presence.

But what is our whole system of Christian Endeavor if it is not a series of unconscious steps up invisible mountains? The prayer meetings, in a sense, are routine affairs; fulfilling the pledge, in our discouraged moments, may seem like a perfunctory obligation; the committees, like the lifeless parts of a machine; but one great object of the Society is to form *habits* of well-doing, habits of confession, of devotion, of service.

Walking itself, after a while, becomes an unconscious act, and moral hill-climbing an unconscious habit.

After all, one does not very often set out to climb the Alps; and, when he gets upon a snow-clad, cloud-capped mountain, he very soon has to come down again. But from these gentle slopes of every-day duty and gentleness and kindness there need be no return. This is the best kind of mountain-climbing, for these steps lead one at last to the top, and into the very presence of God.

III

THE LAND OF WILLIAM TELL

It is strange that a dead hero can dominate for many centuries the land of his adventures. But so it is. France, I imagine, for hundreds of years to come will be Napoleon's land; Sweden will be the kingdom of Gustavus Adolphus, whoever the reigning sovereign may be; and Mexico will always be the province of the brave Hidalgo.

But that a land should be ruled by the memory of a man that never existed, should be dominated by a mythological character, as, the authorities say, was William Tell, is stranger still. Yet it is true that the chief interest, apart from the natural scenery, that attaches to the Vierwaldstättersee, the loveliest lake in the world, perhaps, is due to the supposed adventures of a man that did not live, did not slay the tyrant Gessler, or shoot the apple from his brave boy's head. It is a tribute to the matchless genius of Schiller, and shows how abiding an influence even a tradition of a great and noble life exerts.

The romantic story of William Tell adds just

the element of heroic adventure that this charming lake and country of the Four Forest Cantons of Switzerland need to complete their charms.

At the head of the lake frowns Pilatus, grim and jagged as of yore, when, according to the tradition, Pilate fled hither to wash his accursed hands free of their stains of blood. When he found he could not do this, he threw himself despairing into the dark and gloomy lake near the mountain's top. Further down the lake, much-climbed Rigi, robbed of its mystic terrors, if it ever had any, by the two lines of railway that ascend and take to its summit ceaseless crowds of tourists, raises its precipitous cliffs six thousand feet above the sea, while on the other side of the lake the village of Stanz, with the Stanzerhorn towering above, marks the exploits of Winkelried.

But all the lower end of the lake, where the cantons of Uri, Schwytz, and Unterwalden come together, is, beyond all others, Tell's country. Whether we sail down the winding lake, with the frowning cliffs, some of them snow-clad, towering overhead, and almost meeting above us in places, or travel over the magnificent roads that border the lake, and are frequently cut out of the solid mountain wall of rock, the excursion is equally charming by land or water.

Many of the quaint, low-browed houses, like Stauffacher's in Tell's time, are

> "Emblazoned with painted shields of arms,
> And words of wisdom which the traveller
> Sojourning reads and marvels at their meaning."

Nothing that can add picturesque charm to the scene is wanting. On the right side of the lake, as you go toward Fluellen, high up on the hillside, is Rutli, where the clans came together to plan freedom for Switzerland and death to Austria's tyrannical power. On every side in the springtime flow little waterfalls,

> "The glacier milk
> Which from the fissures trickles foaming down."

Near Rutli is a huge rock rising eighty feet out of the lake, a natural monument, which has most appropriately been dedicated to Schiller and carved with his name in bold letters.

Nearly opposite this on the left is Tell's chapel, a stone shrine built on the verge of the lake and adorned with large and excellent frescos of the stirring events in Tell's life.

Here once every year a service is held, and the hearts of the sturdy Switzers are stirred again to patriotism and love of freedom, which for so many centuries they have maintained.

In the wild storm, you will remember, when Gessler's men could no longer manage the boat, he was obliged to call upon his prisoner for help. Tell was bound and lying in the boat, being carried to the dungeon, "where neither sun nor moon will give thee light," as Gessler assured him.

Taking advantage of the storm and of the fright of the boatman, he steered the boat to this sheltering rock.

> "I breathed a prayer to God for grace, and jamming
> The rudder down with all the force I could,
> I pressed the boat's stern right against this rock;
> Then, quick my weapon seizing, swung myself
> Upon this ledge above me with a bound."

Here on this legendary site stands the chapel to-day. When we visited it, a German cornetist was also making the same pilgrimage; and, turning his silver horn to the open door of the chapel, he softly played, "Nearer, my God, to thee," "a prayer for God's grace" that we could all breathe on that fair, beautiful day, so different from the scene at the time of Tell's adventure on the same spot.

A walk of two miles from Fluellen at the head of the lake, through green pastures which always echo to the cow-bell's tinkle, brings us to the little village of Altdorf, the scene of Tell's most famous exploit. Here a prison was being erected for patriotic spirits such as Tell; and here the hated tyrant Gessler commanded him to shoot the apple from his son's head.

The very spot where Tell stood, according to the story, is marked by a colossal bronze statue of the great archer, and the statue is set off by being placed against a great tower, on whose side is painted a huge picture of the memorable scene.

A public fountain a few yards away is said to mark the spot where the brave Walter Tell stood, with his back against a tree, and the apple on his curly head. As they proposed to bandage his eyes, that he might not watch the arrow's fatal flight, the fearless lad cries out:—

> "Wherefore my eyes? Suppose I'd be flinching
> At shaft from father's hand? I will stand fast
> Awaiting it, nor even wink my eyelids.
> Quick, father, show them thou a marksman art."

At last, after a vain attempt to soften the tyrant's heart, the arrow flies and cleaves the apple to the core, leaving the boy unharmed.

> "That was a shot! 'T will be
> The talk of man down to the latest ages.
>
> "They will relate tales of the archer Tell,
> As long as mountains are enduring."

"What is the use," do you say, "of marking with monument and fountain the legendary scene of heroism? It is but a sentiment to make so much of the mythical Tell's prowess."

Ah! but "the world is ruled by sentiment."

Would that it were ruled still more by such sentiments of patriotic heroism as are stirred by the story of William Tell!

Who can say how much of the spirit of sturdy republicanism and unfaltering love of freedom which the Swiss, more than any people of Europe, have exhibited for five centuries, is due to the story of dauntless William Tell?

IV

A LESSON FROM THE JUNGFRAU

A few days ago I toiled up the Wengern Alp. It was a hard climb of four hours from Lauterbrunnen, but we were repaid for every wearisome step by the magnificent views that burst upon us at every turn.

On one side was rugged, cloud-tipped Murren, down whose furrowed sides poured the Staubbach and half a dozen lesser waterfalls.

Before our eyes were the ever unfolding glories of the Jungfrau and her mighty attendants, the Eiger, the Silberhorn, and the Schneehorn, clad in their dazzling, unsullied garments of driven snow. It was one of the few perfect mornings of this very cloudy summer in Switzerland, and every gigantic, snow-crowned peak was looking its grandest.

As we came to a fork in the path, where the view was beyond all words to express, I stopped a moment to ask some workmen, who were digging a cellar, the way to the Little Scheideck. They politely told me, and at the same time taught me a lesson; for I noticed that from their hole in the ground they could not get the faintest glimpse of the wonderful mountain-peaks.

There they were in the very face and eyes of mountain scenery that you and I, dear fellow traveller, would cross oceans and continents to behold. By taking half a dozen steps out of their circumscribed hole in the ground they could gaze upon such sights as poets have felt powerless to sing and the greatest artists to paint; yet for hours at a time they were oblivious of the Jungfrau and the Silberhorn.

Every few minutes an avalanche would go thundering down the mountain-side with the noise of an express train's roar, while a Niagara of snow could be seen leaping from peak to peak, until it found rest in the valley beneath; but these hardy Switzers did not once turn their heads to see the glorious sight.

Now I have written all this, not to show the stupidity of Swiss peasants or their woful lack of appreciation of the beauties of nature; for you and I, if we spent our lives on the Wengern Alp, would doubtless be just as oblivious to its glories. In fact, it is because you and I are so much like the Wengern Switzers that I have told you about them by way of a parable, that we may see our faces reflected in theirs.

Here are we, living with God in our very midst; but some of us have never seen him, and others have caught only a fragmentary, fleeting glimpse, and then have turned to our digging and delving in the dirt again.

We have but to lift up our spiritual eyes to behold him, and we have never done it. We hear the noise of his avalanches, the thunder of his providences, and we scarcely turn our heads to see whence the providence comes, or to read its meaning.

O the benumbing effect of familiarity and use! The Bible has been in our hands so many years that it has become a commonplace book to us. We have read its precious promises of rest and comfort so many times that these jewels have lost their sparkle, and are but common pebbles.

We are so used to the thought of God as our refuge and strength, our high rock, our impregnable mountain, that in its familiarity we forget its reality and its tremendous truth.

These truths of the reality and the presence of God are the truths that have made men great in all the ages, and these truths are all for us, fellow Christian Endeavorers.

God reveals himself to the common man that will look for him just as truly as to the sage and the prophet, just as those Swiss laborers could see the mighty Jungfrau if they would only climb out of their hole in the ground and turn their heads.

Nay, you need not leave your daily work, digging cellars though it may be. In your cellar, with your hands stained with honest toil, you can see God.

But you must look. That is the one condition. You must look. You must not let usage or familiarity or prejudice shut God away from you, or seal the Bible to your eyes, or stop your ears to the noise of his goings in the world.

Open your eyes to him, and you will say with Jacob, "Surely the Lord is in this place, and I knew it not"; and with Job, "I have heard of thee by the hearing of the ear, but now mine eye seeth thee."

But do you say to me, "Your sermon is quite long already; it is somewhat mystical, and not altogether practical"? Well, I have preached it to myself, and I hope one auditor has been benefited, in any event.

V

CHRISTIAN ENDEAVOR IN SWITZERLAND

Of late, my fellow travellers, we have been across France, through much of Switzerland, and are now for a day at Coblenz on the Rhine, on our way to Berlin, where the second Christian Endeavor convention of Germany opens next week.

Though I am in Germany, my letter to-day must be about Christian Endeavor in Switzerland. The pioneers of genuine Christian Endeavor in Switzerland were the three Murray sisters, of Lausanne. But, a few months since, they went to India to live; and though, as you might be very sure, they have done all they could for the movement in their new home, the cause has languished in Switzerland since their departure.

I was invited, however, to attend two gatherings, one in Zurich and one in Winterthur. Zurich is the largest town in Switzerland, a thriving, Protestant city of one hundred and fifty thousand inhabitants, while Winterthur is a smaller city, but an important railway centre.

Come into one of these meetings with me, for it is typical of my work for Christian Endeavor in all foreign lands, or, rather, in lands where English is not spoken. Let us attend the Zurich meeting together. It is held in St. Anna's Lutheran Church, and an audience of about three hundred Switzers are present, many of them young men and maidens. My interpreter is a pleasant-faced lady, who has spent many years in England. We stand up together in a box pulpit raised high above the congregation.

I say a sentence in English, and she repeats it in German. Another sentence in English, a pause, and its equivalent is given in German. Again a little English, followed by a little German, and during each pause I have time to realize how very unsatisfactory it is to speak in an unknown tongue, while with every breath I say with the apostle, "I had rather speak five words with my understanding, that by my own voice I might teach others also, than ten thousand words in an unknown tongue."

Moreover, there are some Christian Endeavor expressions that are difficult to put into another language. For instance, the very name, "Christian Endeavor," is not easy of translation. The word at first adopted in Germany, "Christliche Bestrebungen," has to some German ears an unpleasant significance of vaulting ambition, instead of the modest, humble meaning that attaches to our word, "Endeavor"; and so the phrase, "Entschiedenes Christenthum," has been recently adopted. Moreover, as you can imagine, "lookout committee," "consecration meeting," "social committee," etc., are not without their difficulties. No wonder that some of these words are "posers," since they have found their way into our latest English dictionaries only since the Christian Endeavor movement has become strong.

However, my interpreter overcomes the difficulties most admirably; the audience listens with exemplary patience, and some have the politeness to tell me after the address that they have enjoyed the evening; and many requests come for literature and further information, with the assurance that some fruit will result in the future.

I describe this meeting with some particularity, for it is a fair sample of much of this seed-sowing in foreign lands. It is no easy task, I assure you. To speak through an interpreter is always a mortification of the flesh to the first speaker, and is anything but an easy task for the interpreter; but "needs must" is a stern taskmaster; and, if it will help on the Master's kingdom through Christian Endeavor, I am quite willing to speak the ten thousand words in an unknown tongue, as I shall probably do nearly every day for seven months to come.

The next day after the meeting in Zurich I

Christian Endeavor in Switzerland

addressed three gatherings in Winterthur, a pastors' conference in the morning at Pastor Ninck's house, a Sunday-school convention in the afternoon, and a popular meeting in the evening. At all these gatherings Pastor Ninck translated for me, and succeeded in interesting the audience, however poor may have been the material he had to translate.

This pastor bears one of the most honored names in Germany, his lamented father having been a minister of renown in Hamburg and an author of note, whose works are known on both sides of the Atlantic. He is thoroughly interested in Christian Endeavor, and feels that it has a mission in Switzerland; and I hope that through his energetic and influential advocacy the Society may find a kindly welcome in this sturdy little republic to whose example and heroism we in the American republic owe so much

VI

GOOD NEWS CONCERNING KRISTNA ENDEAV-
OURFÖRENINGARNAS

CAN you translate from Swedish into English the long word, with its twenty-two letters, which heads this chapter? I imagine you will not have much difficulty, for the first three syllables are familiar, whatever may be said of the last five.

The two words mean nothing more formidable than "Christian Endeavor Unions," which is the subject on which I was asked to speak at the meeting of the Swedish Sunday-school Union in Stockholm on September 19.

Though this was a meeting of the "Sveriges Söndagsskolförbunds," it may with equal propriety be called the first Christian Endeavor convention of Sweden, for our Society was the chief topic discussed, and, of the two days' convention, it occupied the whole of one day and part of the other.

But to begin at the beginning, since we are fellow travellers. We left beautiful Lucerne on the fifteenth of September; for, though the distance to Stockholm is scarcely a thousand miles (about as far as from New York to Chicago), it takes us, with the many delays at customhouses and the slow trains of northern Europe, four days and nights to reach the beautiful capital of Sweden.

We leave the Alps, the fertile plains of Alsace and Lorraine, and the mighty cathedral tower of Strasburg behind us, and then a multitude of busy German cities, until at last we reach Hamburg. Then across the northern peninsula of Germany to Kiel, where Emperor William's Canal was opened with so much pomp and circumstance a few months since. Then by steamer to the flat pastures of Denmark, by rail again to Copenhagen (Kjöbenhavn, if you would spell it as the natives do), by steamer again to Malmö on the Swedish coast, and thence by rail sixteen hours more to Stockholm.

We cannot stop for sight-seeing, except as we get the fleeting but charming views from the car-windows or the steamer's deck, for we are due in Stockholm early Saturday morning, September 19.

At the station to meet us was Bank-president Carlson (it is proper to give a man's business title here in Sweden), who took me at once to his most hospitable home; and, if you had all been with me, a hundred thousand of you, his heart is big enough, if not his house, to take us all in.

There is a peculiar charm about Swedish hospitality that I wish you could all enjoy with me. Every now and then my kind host would stop to shake hands with me, and pat me on the back under the left shoulder-blade in a manner peculiarly Swedish, and say, "Dear Dr. Clark, you are very welcome to Sweden." How could one help feeling at home?

Soon the meetings began. Mr. Carlson, the president of the union; Mr. Bookdealer Palm, the secretary, and his assistant, Mr. Sandberg, are all most hearty friends of Christian Endeavor, and are bound to give it the right of way in this convention.

I am introduced to the executive committee of the Union, an earnest and devoted company of men from all parts of Sweden, and then to the convention as a whole, and in the evening deliver a "föredrag," which is interpreted by Pastor Truvé, of Göteborg, who studied in America for several years, and understands English as well as his native language.

I found the fallow ground well broken up, and the Christian Endeavor seed already planted, and the times ready for just such an occasion as this to give the movement form and momentum.

Mr. Palm, Mr. Sandberg, and others, had already written and spoken much on the subject; a leaflet had been translated and widely circulated; and all that I had to do was to remove a few misapprehensions on the part of some, and show how simple, flexible, and universal the Society is in its operations.

In fact, there are already a large number of young people's societies in Sweden which have received their inspiration from the Christian Endeavor movement, and have adopted in part our principles, especially the committees; but they had not adopted the name or the pledge, and few have prayer meetings. But this convention will go far, I believe, toward establishing and unifying the work on the true basis.

Considerable discussion occurred over the name, but at last it was decided to put the English word right into the heart of the Swedish name, and christen the new organization

KRISTNA ENDEAVOR FÖRENINGEN.

Should they put the "u" in "Endeavor" as the English do, or leave it out as the Americans do? I discreetly kept my mouth shut on this subject, but it was decided to adopt the American spelling, Endeavor, as being more in accord with Swedish usage.

It is rightly felt that this common name will of itself be a bond of union and sympathy between old Sweden in Europe and new Sweden in America.

VII

CONCERNING MUCH WANDERING IN MANY LANDS

Since I last recorded our wanderings, my dear fellow travellers, we have been in many lands,—Sweden, Denmark, Germany, Holland, England, Scotland, Ireland, all in one week. We have been examined at five customhouses, and have crossed two of the most vicious stretches of the Atlantic that you can imagine.

These bits of the North Sea and the German Ocean are always lying in wait for the unsuspecting traveller, with their seasick horrors, but last week they were unusually violent. The "equinoctial gale" was raging; and a terrible gale it was, lashing the sea into a perfect fury and strewing the coast in every direction with wrecks.

During the very height of this terrific storm we were crossing from Denmark to Germany, a seven hours' journey; and again the next night from Holland to England, seven hours more, in a still more violent tempest. The way those little steamers stood first on their heads and then on their heels, and then, for a change, seemed to turn over on their sides, and balance themselves on each elbow alternately, went beyond my powers of description.

Every now and then a huge wave would strike the steamer with a report like that of a cannon. One of these waves broke in the port light directly over my berth, and flooded my bunk, but fortunately did no other damage. Perhaps you will be glad, when you read these words, that " we " are travelling together only *figuratively.*

But these long nights of peril and discomfort are forgotten when London is reached, and in the familiar home of those good friends of all Christian Endeavorers, Mr. and Mrs. Waters, we meet the members of the London Council, of which Rev. F. B. Meyer is president.

Since reaching London we have been attending a succession of great Christian Endeavor meetings, which you can imagine, but which I find it hard to describe. The welcome meeting in the Tabernacle (Spurgeon's) filled that magnificent auditorium to the topmost gallery; yet there had been no public advertising and not a line of notice in the papers. Mr. Meyer presided, and spoke most enthusiastic words for Christian Endeavor as a spiritual force; and the welcoming address by Mr. Fleming was beyond all description kind and cordial. To my mind the great significance of the event lay in its demonstration of the strong hold that Christian Endeavor has taken of the Christian public of London. It was far more than a personal matter. It was an occasion that told the public that Christian Endeavor had come to London to stay as a permanent, aggressive religious factor.

The day following, Sunday, was a busy day. In the morning and afternoon, at Bloomsbury Chapel, one of London's famous Baptist churches, and in the evening at Mr. Meyer's church, Christ Church, of Westminster Bridge Road.

This great church, as many of you know, was built in part by American friends in Dr. Newman Hall's time, and is a vast and ever increasing force for good in London life under the pastorate of that saintly man whose helpful words are read by so many of you.

Glasgow, the great commercial metropolis of the Scots, was our next stopping-place, and the home of our dear friend Mr. Pollock our delightful haven. Here we met many of the officers of the Scottish Union, and afterward a great public meeting was held in beautiful St. Andrew's Hall, which housed, I suppose, fully four thousand Glasgow Endeavorers that night.

There I saw the badge banner for the greatest proportionate increase in societies, which Scotland won last year. There, too, as in London, most kind and generous words were spoken, which told of the strong hold that the Endeavor cause is gaining on the Scotch as well as the English heart.

On this evening, too, was launched *Scottish Endeavour*, a bright, breezy, yet substantial, sixteen-page monthly, edited by Mr. Pollock and Mr. Fleming.

Now I am in Belfast, the great metropolis of northern Ireland, where the best Christian Endeavor convention that Ireland has ever known, and one of the best I ever attended anywhere, is in progress.

Here are Mr. Lamont and Mr. Montgomery, whom you remember at Boston, and Mr. Newman Hall, of Montreal and Belfast, who is about to go to Montreal again for a few days, I am informed, on a "*home* mission." Ireland has designs on the banner that Scotland holds this year. Keep your eye on the Emerald Isle.

I cannot omit a reference to the intense, burning indignation that is felt everywhere against the Sultan and his government, or misgovernment. In every speech this indignation blazes forth, and at every meeting resolutions are passed calling upon Lord Salisbury's government to end the rule of the Turk and thus to mend Armenia.

I ought also to have said that before I crossed the stormy North Sea to England, a hopeful meeting was held in Rotterdam in the interests of Christian Endeavor, the first ever held on Holland's soil. From this seed-sowing I hope for a future harvest.

VIII

FREDERICK BROTHERTON MEYER

A Man That Walks with God

One of the men heretofore mentioned in this volume should occupy a larger space than a line of passing allusion, so many of my fellow travellers have been blessed unspeakably by his written and spoken words.

Frederick Brotherton Meyer is no stranger to most of you. You have drawn inspiration from him, for he *speaks* to you through the printed page as few men are able to speak. His words are no dead things. They glow and live with his own personality. If you know thoroughly his writings, you know the man.

Yet it is pleasant to see an old friend in his own environment. The jewel loses nothing by reason of its setting.

Christ Church, Westminster Bridge Road, London, is one of the churches that lives and breathes. A magnificent structure it is, of gray stone. It is of peculiar interest to Americans by reason of its imposing "Lincoln tower," which, during the pastorate of Dr. Newman Hall, was built by money raised in America.

This church has had a notable succession of eminent ministers, the renowned Rowland Hill being its first pastor. In all its appointments —its audience-room, its Sunday-school class-rooms, its lecture hall, and in all its smaller committee rooms—it is complete, according to the most modern ideas of ecclesiastical architecture. But we are most interested in seeing its pastor in his study. A beautiful room is this study, but beautiful by reason of its associations and the pictures that hang upon the wall, and because of its living inmate, more than by reason of any rich furnishings or drapery. Here, as is natural, hangs an oil painting of Rowland Hill; another picture is of Newman Hall, while a marble bust of Dr. Hall stands in one corner.

Here, too, is a large photograph of Mr. Spurgeon, while upon a table near by stands a speaking likeness of Dr. A. J. Gordon, of Boston, a man for whom Mr. Meyer expresses the profoundest reverence and affection.

Another framed relic that makes the room attractive is a leaf from the diary of McCheyne, together with a pressed flower that McCheyne himself picked at Palestine.

But the living occupant attracts us more than all the worthies that hang upon the wall. A man of medium height and rather slender build, whose somewhat sparse hair is brushed back from a full forehead, sits in the easy-chair before me, talking in low but most earnest tones. His whole manner is as far from sepulchral gloom as it is from trivial levity. He impresses you as meaning every word he says. There is one theme that above all others gives a pathos and a richness to his voice, and that is the love of Christ and the importance of a life fully given to him.

"Won't you tell me a little about your experience of full consecration, Mr. Meyer?" I said.

"Most gladly," he replied. "It is the one thing in my life that is worth talking about, if anything is. I had accomplished some good, I believe, before this experience, and was not altogether a failure as a minister; but I had not the power with men or with God that I desired. There was one stumbling-block in the way, one thing I had to yield, one affection that I had to root out of my heart; but, when the surrender was fully made and I gave up absolutely everything to God, the way became clear and bright.

"I do not mean that everything was revealed to me suddenly. New apartments of the riches of God's grace are constantly being opened to me, but then I received the key that opened the outer door, and all the other doors swing inward as I come to them.

"The two sayings that impressed me most deeply," he went on to say, "were, in the first place, one that was overheard by Moody as he walked in Phœnix Park in Dublin. He heard one man saying to another, as they walked behind him, 'The world does not yet know what God can accomplish through a fully consecrated man.'

"The other saying that greatly influenced my life was Hudson Taylor's remark to me one day, —'God told me that he was going to evangelize inland China, and that he would do it through me, if I would only walk by his side.'

"Often and often have I thought of these words," said Mr. Meyer, "and great has been their influence upon my life. Tell the young people," he continued, "to read and reread and then to read again the Gospel of John, and see how our Lord was *used* by the Father, how God spoke through him and to him, and how he was simply the moving will of God. There is our example in this as in all things."

"But do you always have an abiding peace and joy and confidence?" I said. "Are there no ups and downs in your religious experience?"

"Well," he replied, "I am not a man of ecstasies, or of exalted heights or abysmal depths. I do not think much about my emotions or my feelings, but simply try to do what

God would have me do, and there is a satisfaction and peace in my life which passes understanding."

Great as is the congregation to which Mr. Meyer preaches on Sunday, it is a vastly greater congregation to which he preaches through the printed page.

Not only are his sermons widely reported, but he is undoubtedly the most prolific writer of devotional books and booklets of the present generation, perhaps the most voluminous writer of devotional literature that the world has ever known. Moreover, there is a uniformity of excellence about his work which is most remarkable. He has written very few dull pages, and fewer still weak pages. He is a master of simple, lucid, musical English. He never descends to goody-goody talk, or to cheap sentimentality. There is much of piety, but very little pietism, in his pages; much religion, but no religiosity. His is also a manly and virile style as well as poetic and musical. His illustrations are drawn from the very widest range, and show a large acquaintance with the literature of the ages. Yet it is very evident that the Bible is the chief source of his inspiration and his power. He is above all an *expositor*. He often takes a common biblical phrase, which, because of its very familiarity, we pass by as we would a pebble in the street, and in a few sentences of comment he causes it to glow and sparkle like a diamond of the first water.

For instance, to illustrate his constant illumination of biblical passages, as we were talking together, he said: "O, I have such a fear of being a castaway! Supposing you and I should become in Paul's sense of the word 'castaways,' what a dreadful thing it would be! Now I do not think," he went on to say, "that Paul meant that he was in danger of being cast away from the presence of God, and shut out of heaven, but that he was in danger of rendering himself unfit for God's use, just as we cast aside a pen when it will no longer write, or a bicycle when it becomes worn in its bearings and useless, so Paul feared that the time might come when God could no longer use him for his work; then he would be cast to one side and some fitter instrument be chosen. In this sense the thought comes upon me like a dreadful nightmare sometimes, What if I, too, should become a tool that God could not use, a poor, broken castaway?"

"But how do you manage," I continued, "to accomplish so much work, to write so many books, for something new from your pen comes from the press every few weeks?"

"It is only by keeping at it," he replied, "by using what time I have, and because of a faculty of concentration. I write on the cars, on the trams, wherever I have a few moments of leisure, and I find that I can always take up the train of thought where it is broken off. My mind seems to work right on in the same line, and I can finish out a sentence that I began yesterday, and carry out the thought without a break."

But I cannot linger longer over this visit. It was not a formal interview; neither of us was in the mood of professional writers or newspaper men. We talked together for a little as brother with brother. It was my great privilege to look for a few moments into the clear, transparent depths of a great and good man's soul. I thank God for the glimpse I have gained, and wish that all who read his works would see behind the writings a pure, unselfish, modest, devoted, and holy consecrated life.

IX

THE PLOUGHMAN POET—1796-1896

One of the incidental events in our visit to Glasgow briefly alluded to in a previous chapter was an hour or two spent in the remarkable Burns Exhibition which marked the centennial of the death of the great poet. My visit was made under the happy guidance of the Rev. John Pollock who is a great lover of the Ploughman Poet and who knows his Burns by heart. Nothing is wanting to make this exhibition a memorable one and unique beyond all others of its kind.

Here are brought together, from private collections and public museums, a multitude of objects bearing upon the life of Scotia's bard. The catalogue itself, which records the objects to be seen, is a portly volume of four hundred and eighty-six large pages; and if there is anything which the lover of Burns fails to find in these pages we have not discovered it.

The pictures in this exhibition naturally attracted our attention first. Perhaps the most famous of these is the original portrait of Burns by Alexander Nasmyth, of which there are two replicas and several copies. None of the copies, however, have the beauty and pathetic outlines of the great original.

Another notable picture represents the meeting of Burns and Scott on the only occasion when they were ever brought together. This was at the house of Professor Fergusson, when Scott was a mere boy. Burns had been affected to tears by some lines from an unknown poet under the print of a soldier lying dead on the snow, with his widow and dog beside him. No one in the room could tell who wrote the lines except the boy, Walter Scott, who volunteered the information; and Burns rewarded him with a kind look which Scott never forgot.

Innumerable paintings and engravings have been inspired by the poet's work, and the walls of this great exhibition are hung with the painter's conception of the poet's thought.

"Tam o' Shanter" naturally has inspired the greatest number of prints and paintings, and by more than one large canvas we are reminded how

> "The doubling storm roars through the woods;
> The lightnings flash from pole to pole;
> Near and more near the thunders roll;
> When, glimmering through the groaning trees,
> Kirk Alloway seemed in a bleeze."

"The Cotter's Saturday Night" shares with "Tam o' Shanter" the honor of inspiring most frequently the artist's brush; but many of the minor poems have also been illustrated by great masters of the pallet.

The portraits of many of the people, too, whom Burns immortalized hang upon these walls. Even those who are alluded to in no complimentary terms are here found. James Elphinstone, for instance, of whom Burns wrote,—

> "O thou whom Poetry abhors!
> Whom Prose had turned out-of-doors."

Here, too, is the picture of William Creech, the poet's publisher,—

> "A little upright, pert, tart, tripping wight,
> And still his precious self his dear delight;
> Who loves his own smart shadow in the streets,
> Better than e'er the fairest she he meets."

Many another author, perhaps, can enter into Burns's inmost feelings as he reads these withering lines, though he be not the master of such a picturesque and varied assortment of adjectives.

Of even more interest than the pictures upon the walls are the precious manuscripts, carefully preserved from moth and rust behind transparent glass. Here we find "Holy Willie's Prayer," which we do not wonder grated so harshly upon the Calvinistic sensibilities of many of Burns's countrymen:—

> "O Thou, wha in the heavens dost dwell,
>   Wha, as it pleases best thysel',
> Sends ane to heaven and ten to hell,
>   A' for thy glory,
> And no for ony guid or ill
>   They 've done afore thee!"

One of the most interesting manuscripts is written, not upon the coarse and time-stained paper which often tells of the poet's poverty, but upon a pane of glass which has been carefully removed from its window-frame and preserved for posterity to read. On this glass Burns scratched with diamond point the famous thirty-two lines, beginning :—

> "Thou whom chance may hither lead,
> Be thou clad in russet weed,
> Be thou deckt in silken stole,
> Grave these maxims on thy soul.
> Life is but a day at most
> Sprung from night in darkness lost."

A bottle in a tin box in this unique exhibition contains a bookworm, with the inscription written below :—

> "Through and through the inspired leaves,
>   Ye maggots make your windings;
> But O, respect his lordship's taste,
>   And spare his golden bindings."

We must not pass by the multitudinous editions of Burns's works. Were there nothing else in this exhibition, these editions alone would make it memorable, and would show the wonderfully enduring hold which the poet of the ploughshare has upon the hearts of mankind. Case after case is filled with editions of the poet's work, sent forth by hundreds of publishers and in many languages. They are of all sizes, too, from the tiny thumbnail edition which can be read only with a magnifying-glass to the portly folio.

Our own country is represented in this collection by sixty-seven different editions, one of which was issued in Hartford, one in Salem, one in Wilmington, two in Baltimore, eighteen in Boston, twenty-one in New York, and twenty-one in Philadelphia. Of course the editions printed in England are literally numbered by the hundreds, and all this within a hundred years from the death of the poet.

There are a multitude of other interesting relics which I cannot take space to mention, among them a large armchair loaned by Queen Victoria, made from the beams of Alloway Kirk. On the inlaid brass in the back of this chair is engraved the whole of "Tam o' Shanter"; and it is in itself, apart from its royal associations, a beautiful work of art.

The secret of the poet's power, so wonderfully exemplified by this centennial exhibition, a power which seems to be increasing as the years go by, is not far to seek. Every lover of

Burns would give a somewhat different explanation, perhaps, and though each explanation might be partial, each would be true. One will find the source of his power in his stalwart patriotism and love of country, a patriotism which touches a responsive chord in the heart of every man in every clime who to himself hath said, "This is my own, my native land."

> "An early wish (I mind its power)
> I had, and to my latest hour
>   It still shall heave my breast;
> That I, for poor auld Scotland's sake,
> Some useful plan, or beuk could make,
>   Or sing a sang at least."

Another will explain the mighty grip which he has upon the heart of mankind by his sturdiness of character which seems to give a strength and vigor to every slightest poem, a sturdy self-respect which never toadied to the great or rich in whatever straits he found himself. Burns once wrote:—

"However inferior, now or afterward, I may rank as a poet, one honest virtue to which few poets can pretend I trust I shall ever claim as mine. To no man, whatever his station in life, or his power to serve me, have I ever paid a compliment at the expense of truth."

His uncompromising love of common people and common things, his unswerving democracy when democracy was by no means a popular "fad," will ever endear him to the common people.

But above all he is Nature's poet and always keeps close to Nature's heart. In this lies the great secret of his charm and power. So often has this been said that to repeat it is wearisome; but it has never been better said than by the anonymous author who thus describes him:—

> "The Simple Bard, unbroke by rules of Art,
> He pours the wild effusions of the heart;
> And if inspir'd, 't is Nature's pow'rs inspire;
> Hers all the melting thrill and hers the kindling fire."

X

THREE THOUSAND MILES IN GERMANY

Our three weeks' campaign in the "Fatherland" involved something like three thousand miles of travel back and forth, and up and down, crisscrossing Germany in all directions. Meetings have been held not only in German Switzerland on the edge of the German Empire, and in the great cities of Berlin and Hamburg and Breslau and Dresden, and in Halle and Leipsic, but in most of the principal provinces of Germany as well, in Pomerania and Silesia, in East Prussia and West Prussia, in Saxony and Hanover, and in Hesse Nassau also.

The last four meetings have been among the most interesting of all. In Cassel may be said to be the headquarters of Christian Endeavor for Germany. Here is the largest society of all, with about one hundred and twenty members. Moreover, both young men and women are found in this society. This is a startling innovation for Germany. One would almost think, to hear the common remarks on this subject, that it was about the most immodest and dangerous thing in the world for young men and women to come together in a prayer meeting. The great restrictions under which the fair sex is placed in all such matters in Germany will undoubtedly prove a decided hindrance to the work of Christian Endeavor.

But the customs of the centuries cannot be altered in a single day, or the prejudices of a thousand years dissipated like the morning mist. Though I find many, pastors and others, who would like greater freedom of social intercourse between the young men and the young women of their churches, and feel that the unconstrained mingling in religious meetings would make for purity and righteousness and the advancement of the kingdom of God, even they cannot bring it about in their own churches.

Still, as I say, here in Cassel is a genuine mixed Christian Endeavor society, and a most earnest and aggressive one, if I may judge from all appearances. At any rate, I am sure that the members show their colors, for most of the young ladies, I noticed, wore huge silver C. E. monograms almost as large as one of our cartwheel dollars.

The next morning early, I was off for Wiesbaden, the famous watering-place near the Rhine, where the empress of Germany has been this past summer, with her royal retinue. No wonder she goes there, for it is one of the loveliest towns in Germany, and its waters are famous throughout the world.

But of more interest to us is to know that here, too, is a fine Christian Endeavor society in the church of the beloved and honored Pastor Ziemendorff. I do not know when I have enjoyed an evening more than the one in Wiesbaden.

This society is largely composed of young ladies, but the sterner sex are not excluded, and I saw at least four of them whose white ribbon badges proclaimed that they are members of the Wiesbaden Society.

But if there were few young men to lend their manly dignity, a society of such young ladies would be a strong and notable one in any land.

After the public meeting, where my address was translated by Pastor Ziemendorff, and by an American physician of the town, an after meeting of the society and a few of its friends was held. At this gathering reports were given from all branches of the society work. Some of the young ladies spoke in German, and some in excellent English, and, as I told them, I had to rub my eyes to make sure, as I heard the encouraging story of the year's work, whether I was in England or America or Germany. Afterward, Miss Ziemendorff translated a brief address of mine with the utmost fluency. Altogether it was a delightful and memorable experience.

The next morning, almost before daylight, I started to traverse a large slice of Germany once more, and evening found me in the great university town of Halle. The meeting-place was the hall of the famous school founded in the last century by the devout Francke, one of the most godly men that ever lived in Germany. Starting with nothing but an overmastering faith and unbounded zeal, the huge buildings, the flourishing school, and the vast influence of his work, not only in Halle, but throughout Germany, testify in the strongest manner to the power of faith and prayer.

Many of the schoolboys were present at the meeting, as well as the director of the great Institute. Both here and in Leipsic, a number of students from the universities attended, including many Americans, and it was my pleasant privilege to greet Endeavorers from all parts of the United States and Canada. The hospitable cordiality of these kind friends I shall not soon forget.

In these two places, Pastor Simsa, the prison chaplain of Halle, was my interpreter, and a better none could ever wish to have. Thus has come to an end this long series of Christian Endeavor meetings in Germany. In almost every instance have I been surprised at the large audiences that have gathered, and at the evident interest manifested. Still, there are many and mountainous difficulties in the way of Christian Endeavor in Germany, and what the result of this seed-sowing will be, only the future years will tell. May some **seed** spring **up** and bear fruit unto eternal life.

XI

TWO FAMOUS GERMANS IN THE CLASSROOM

Wellhausen and Harnack

To-day let us catch a glimpse of student life in Germany. Let me try to picture for you two striking figures of the German classroom, in these end-of-the-century days. I will not speak of their orthodoxy or heterodoxy, or the hair-splitting differences of the philosophy which they advocate, but simply give a first and surface impression of the way in which they strike an American on his first introduction to their classrooms.

Let us go to Göttingen first. An old middle-of-the-era city is this, with crooked, narrow streets and beetle-browed houses placarded with famous names, showing that Bismarck and Longfellow and Bancroft and many another celebrity once dwelt in them. The town is surrounded by an ancient wall, now entirely unused except as a promenade,—the "Indian Ridge" of Göttingen. All my readers who have been Andover students will understand this allusion.

There are only about twenty-six thousand people in the city and the students constitute one-twenty-sixth part of the population, giving them a far more predominant and conspicuous place in the town than they occupy in Halle or Berlin, or the larger university cities of Germany, where, though the students are more numerous, they are swallowed up to a larger extent in the vaster population. Many of the students, though by no means all of them, belong to the different corps which are distinguished by the most brilliant of caps, red, green, blue, or purple, a headgear which is surpassed for ridiculous absurdity only by the jaunty little red cap which the English Tommy Atkins balances in a most precarious way over his right ear, holding the strap thereof apparently in his mouth, lest it should at any moment topple down from its insecure perch. Most of these corps students are scarred and seamed like veterans of a hundred battles, as indeed they are, for they are obliged, on pain of expulsion from the corps, to fight at least six duels a year. Some of the faces are perfectly hideous with the deep and brutal scars of which their owners are so proud.

But here is a handsome university lecture hall where almost all the lectures, except those in medicine and chemistry, are given. Before the hour for the lecture arrives it is thronged with students hurrying to the different class-rooms, for punctuality at lectures seems to be one of the virtues of the average university student. We take our seat on one of the long benches, with a desk in front of us carved with the names and initials of many generations of students, together with various symbols and devices which tell of wandering thoughts. Evidently the minds of the students are not always on high theology or lost altogether in the fog of metaphysical speculation, for the names of "Emma" and "Lisa" and "Ida" and various other feminine appellations appear upon the much-carved desks.

The students are all in their places, when the door opens, and, with a quick, nervous tread, the professor enters. It is the famous Wellhausen, who many timid souls have feared would shake the very foundations of our faith and uproot all our traditionary views of the word of God. A man of stout and muscular build, with iron-gray hair and beard, he is by no means fierce or malevolent looking. Hurriedly entering the room, he hastily throws off his overcoat, steps onto the platform behind his desk, and begins to talk in a most nonchalant and indifferent sort of a way almost before he has hung his coat upon its appropriate peg.

This studied indifference of *entrée* and exit seems to be affected by many German professors. I say "affected" advisedly, for no man can really be quite so utterly indifferent and unconscious of all his surroundings as many German professors appear. No word of kindly salutation to the class, no prayer such as we are all accustomed to in our theological seminaries before the lecture begins, nothing but a jump into the subject, *in medias res*, and a talk at railroad speed until the three-quarters of an hour are exhausted, when, with equal abruptness, he puts on his coat and hat, talking up to the last minute, and leaves the room almost before the echo of his last word dies away. The whole attitude of the average German theological professor seems to be, "Hear me if you can, but it makes very little difference to me whether you do or not." As to having any personal interest in the individual student, it seems to be furthest from his conception.

In fact, Professor Wellhausen rarely seems to lecture to his students, but directs most of his attention to a crack in the floor about eight feet from the base of the platform on which he stands. As this crack is on the right hand side of the desk, near the back wall of the lecture-room, the students can rarely catch more than a glimpse of a somewhat sharp profile, with a good view of the right ear. Sometimes he turns squarely around with his back to the students and his face to the wall ; sometimes he lifts his eye aloft and fixes it upon a spot in the ceiling, but inevitably the crack in the floor attracts his attention once more and he brings his eyes back to their favorite resting-place.

Just now Wellhausen lectures chiefly on philological subjects, and the heavy guns of his battery are not turned as formerly upon the books of Moses. Whether it is owing to a lack of interest in the subjects on which he discourses, or to his uninteresting style, or to the fact that much of his best work has been published, many of his lectures are attended by very few students, the one which I have described attracting less than a dozen, if I remember correctly.

But it must not be supposed that all German professors adopt this nonchalant, indifferent style. Let us go into Harnack's lecture-room, for instance, in the University of Berlin. Here we find an entirely different state of affairs. There are at least two hundred and fifty or three hundred students present, among whom are nearly a score of Americans, to hear the great authority on church history. We leave our overcoats in the hall outside, and, if we are especially anxious to resume them again when we go out, we chain them to the wall with long steel chains and heavy padlocks which conveniently hang from every hook, for overcoat thieves are both numerous and wily at the door of this theological lecture hall. The room is so full that we are obliged to take the very front seat and literally sit at the feet of the great lecturer.

Scarcely has the last student taken his place, when the door opens once more, and a tall, wiry man, with a thin, scattering mustache and hair brushed straight back from his forehead, enters the room. He is ill-dressed and looks underfed, and we at first think he is one of the poor theologues who is working his way through the university, spending more for midnight oil than for oatmeal porridge. But he mounts the platform instead of taking his seat with the rest of us, and, after a pleasant word of greeting, begins his lecture, for this is none other than the celebrated Harnack. There was nothing of the indifferent "take-it-or-leave-it" air about him.

He soon warms to his subject, and evidently is thoroughly interested himself while seeking to interest his pupils. He gesticulates freely and appropriately. His eyes sparkle, and now and then he runs his fingers through his long hair, pushing it back from his ample forehead. At times he becomes decidedly eloquent, and sallies of wit frequently bring a broad grin to the faces of the eager students, who are diligently pushing their pens to keep up with his torrent of words. Evidently Harnack does not despise the graces of oratory and is not afraid to make his lecture interesting as well as instructive. He seems to have very few notes before him and seldom refers to them. Being too much confined by the narrow platform he frequently comes down onto the lower step; returning he seats himself upon the arm of his professorial chair, balancing himself in a most insecure way until we become so anxious for fear it will topple over and land him in an undignified sprawl upon the floor that we almost forget to listen to his eloquent periods.

To look at it from a material view, if we may be pardoned for so doing, it is well worth the lecturer's while to make his lectures interesting, for he receives, in addition to the somewhat meagre salary paid by the state, a large percentage of the students' fees, something like $5.00 for each of the three hundred students who take this course. All Andover students of the olden days naturally compare every new lecturer whom they hear with that prince of instructors and king of the lecture-room, Professor Park. Who of us will ever forget the eagerness with which we looked forward to those rare literary treats? Who does not remember the human interest with which every dry theological theme was lighted up? Who of us cannot recall the gleam of shrewd humor which used to come into that marvellous face before the lips uttered some sharp witticism or told some extraordinarily good story? Was there ever an instructor who so impressed himself upon his students, or so affected all their modes of thought as did Professor Park?

In these respects Professor Harnack, of all German professors, seems to have more in common with the great preacher of Andover Hill than any one whom I have ever heard.

Speaking of the inevitable tendency to run after new and brilliant luminaries, as illustrated in Professor Weiss's career, Professor Harnack said to a friend of mine: "It comes to all of us sooner or later. It will come to me as well as to the rest. I shall lose my popularity and my students one of these days. The night cometh, the night of decadence and unpopularity, as well as the night of death. It becomes us all to work while our day lasts." Surely the prosaic minister of the simple gospel could utter no more sensible or practical truth than this. For the great scholar, as for the humblest worker, the night cometh. Let us work while it is called to-day.

XII

SOME THINGS IN GERMANY WORTH COPYING

During these weeks in which we have been zigzagging together across the "Fatherland," stopping each night in a new place for a new meeting, I have kept my eyes open for hints and suggestions that might be of use in the home-land across the sea.

It is needless, perhaps, to say that there are many things in our religious life that I believe it would be vastly advantageous to our friends here to copy, and some things here that I should not wish to see copied at home; for instance, the big mugs of foaming beer and the lighted cigars over which Christian Endeavor is often discussed by the ministers and the young men in the Young Men's Christian Associations of Germany.

However, I have not come in the rôle of a critic, but more as a friend and admirer of the land of Luther, to find what good things I can learn.

One of these good things, which I find in almost every city, is a Christian hotel or hospiz, as it is called. Almost every city of considerable size in Germany has a hospiz. Often it is in connection with the Young Men's Christian Association of the city. Sometimes, as in Dresden and Berlin and Stettin, it is a fine, large, handsomely furnished hotel, which would do credit to any metropolis. At other times it is a more modest edifice; but always the rooms are clean, the feather beds, under which one sleeps without any intervening upper sheet, are warm and downy, and the fare is abundant and substantial. In every room is a Bible, and Scripture mottoes and pictures of Bible scenes adorn the walls.

The price asked is not particularly cheap; but neither is it high, and you feel that you are getting all you pay for. The servants are allowed to take no fees, which of itself is a great relief to a travelling American. Every morning, at eight or half past, prayers are held for fifteen minutes in the salon, which are attended by all the servants and by as many of the guests as desire to go.

Why should not such hotels be established in all our cities? The travelling Christian public must be far larger in America than in Germany, and many persons would patronize such a hospiz if it were well kept and could compete in prices with the ordinary hotels of the city. I do not mean a cheap and shabby boarding-house, of doubtful cleanliness and more than doubtful comfort, such as are some of our so-called "temperance hotels," but a genuine, self-respecting, first-class, reasonable-priced hotel. I believe that such a hospiz would be a financial success as well as a boon for the religious public. Who will be the first to attempt the venture in America?

Another thing that I have liked in Germany is the larger use of religious pictures and statues than we are accustomed to at home. There are two works of art of which I see copies in almost every home that I enter in Germany, whether rich or poor, high or low. One is a reproduction of Thorwaldsen's beautiful statue of Christ, the original of which stands in the old Frue Kirke in Copenhagen; and the other is a copy of Plockhorst's beautiful painting of "Christ the Consoler," in which our Lord is represented in a wonderfully gracious and benignant attitude, reaching down to help a poor, burdened sinner who drags himself to his feet. No words can describe the pathetic charm of this picture, or the gracious dignity of the statue.

Sometimes the reproduction is very small and cheap, and costs but a few pfennigs. At other times it is a large and finished production, costing many marks. Such a picture and such a statue would prove a benediction in every home. The sweet and gentle eyes would follow us about our tasks through the day, and would make more real the presence that is not far from every one of us. There are, of course, many other famous religious pictures, of which photographic reproductions could be had for a very small sum, which would greatly beautify our homes and in many instances raise the whole tone of family life.

Another custom that I have liked in the family life of Germany is the almost universal returning of thanks after meals in addition to grace before meat. I like also the custom of having each one at the end of the meal shake hands with every other, and say, " Gesegnete Mahlzeit," a contraction for " Ich wünsche Ihnen gesegnete Mahlzeit," which being interpreted means, " May the dinner agree with you," or " I wish you a good dinner," or " a good appetite." Often the father and mother and children kiss one another, making it an expression of family affection as well as a mere formal greeting. Sometimes the whole family together with invited guests join hands around the table, while they say to one another, " Gesegnete Mahlzeit." Even at the boarding-house where I am lodging, as each one of the many boarders comes into the dining-room, he salutes the others with a pleasant " Mahlzeit," and on going out once more " Mahlzeits " everybody.

One more custom of German life, of which I will speak, is a greater seeming reverence for the word of God. When the Scripture lesson is read in church, the whole congregation rises and stands throughout the reading, and again when the text is read. It seems as if they indeed heard God speak to them, and would do him reverence by their very attitude. I think there is just as much reverence for the word of God with us, but we do not have so happy a way of showing it.

At the close of the service, too, there is always a reverent pause for silent prayer. This custom many of our churches at home have adopted, but why not all? It is certainly more seemly and reverent than a scramble for overcoats and overshoes, and a hasty exit almost before the benediction is spoken. I wish that not only every preaching-service, but that every church prayer meeting and Christian Endeavor service, might close with such a quiet moment for silent prayer. Nothing would more conduce to godly reverence and a fitting impression of the sanctity of the time and place.

XIII

NAPLES BY NIGHT

FROM Germany our duties in behalf of Christian Endeavor called us to India and Africa *via* the Land of the Pyramids. One of the most interesting cities that can be visited on the long journey from Berlin to Alexandria is Naples, our port of embarkation for the Orient. Whether Naples is more picturesque by day or by night, it is difficult to determine. Arriving very early in the morning, expecting a little later the same day to take the steamer of the Florio Rubbatino Company for Egypt, I was coolly informed, after several hours of anxious waiting, that the "Adria" would not sail until the next day, twenty-four hours after her advertised time; so I had a chance to see Naples by night as well as by day.

To tell the truth, she is interesting enough in any hour of the twenty-four to make even a forced sojourn quite endurable.

I know a small boy who in going through the streets of Naples just at dawn would remark, "It's funny how many queer things you see when you have n't got your gun." So it is.

The city is not stirring, though it is almost

broad daylight, for the Neapolitans are late risers; but it is very evidently the milkman's hour. Here he is, out in full force; and here are his living milk-carts, which he drives before him. No dead thing of wood and iron is his milk-cart, but a flock of long-haired, big-uddered goats, which have been trained docilely to turn into any back alley or through any narrow doorway when he gives the word of command.

Moreover, his milk-carts have the advantage of being quite able and willing to mount a steep flight of stairs to the upper story where their cargo is often discharged. Sometimes the milkman drives a cow instead of a flock of shaggy goats, and, whenever he is hailed and handed a receptacle, he fills it directly from the natural fount. These milkmen get very expert, and I have seen one with the greatest dexterity filling a long-necked, narrow-mouthed pint bottle without losing a drop.

Of course there must be some one to receive the lacteal fluid, though it *is* early in the morning; and high up on the balconies of the tall houses, four stories from the ground, you will see a frouzy woman come out with a basket, a tumbler, and a long rope. In the basket she will place her tumbler, to its handle tie the rope, and by this means lower her receptacle to the ground. The milkman will take out the tumbler and the few centesimi which the basket also contains, and fill the glass to the brim, when the maid will pull it up to the top again.

But Naples is beginning to wake, and it is an awakening indeed; for among all noisy cities in the world, I believe she will take the palm. With the first yawn and stretch every one in Naples seems to begin to yell (there is no other word for it), and keeps up this lung-splitting exercise until midnight brings partial repose.

The cabbies are perhaps the greatest sinners in this respect. If they spy a possible fare a quarter of a mile away, they begin to shout at him to attract his attention, and crack their long whips in a most vicious and irritating way. In the populous streets it seems as if a succession of pistol-shots were going off around your ears from dawn to dark. The shoeblacks seek to attract your attention by pounding vigorously on their blocks; the fruit-sellers bawl out their wares in the manner that has been made so familiar by their countrymen at home; the dealers in prickly-pears shout out the virtues of their luscious fruit; the venders of hot chestnuts scream a description of their warm and mealy "castaneas"; and the newsmen, for boys evidently have not lung power enough for this trade, split your ears with "Roma-a," "Tribuna-a," etc., with the last syllable always indefinitely prolonged and emphasized.

When all these venders gather together under the great dome of the beautiful Victor Emmanuel arcade in the centre of the city, and the lofty arches ring with the varied yells, the pandemonium-like effect is indescribable. Babel becomes a living reality.

The narrow lanes of Naples, many of them mere flights of stone steps leading from the lower town to the upper, are fearfully dirty, but exceedingly picturesque. Here everything is going on. Boys are sleeping on the sidewalk in long rows. Women are cooking the dinner in bubbling caldrons of hot oil. Others are combing their children's heads most attentively and minutely, as monkeys are often seen to treat their offspring. In fact, the "Naples hunt" is always in progress. Shoemakers are cobbling most disreputable old scraps of leather, which bear some resemblance to shoes. Fishwives are dispensing mussels and snails and live eels. Gardeners are disposing of leeks, onions, and garlic. Tailors are plying their trade. All kinds of hucksters are peddling small wares. Families are eating dinner. Wayfarers are gorging themselves with vermicular-looking edibles at the macaroni stands. In fact, everything that one can imagine is taking place here in the broad glare and publicity of the hot Italian sun.

But my title promises some night scenes of Naples, and I find the daylight view so interesting that I have little room left for a Gerard Dow picture, even if I could paint one.

At night, however, Naples is very much the same as by day, only more so. The noises, the gay, half-barbaric costumes of the women, the glare of the innumerable flares that mark the provision-booths and little shops, are only emphasized and not subdued by the deepening of the early twilight.

Now come with me to this open street that skirts the harbor, and look off toward that black, towering cone that rears itself beyond the bay. I do not need to tell you that it is dread Vesuvius.

We have been to look at it many times during the day; but by daylight only a cloud of smoke can be seen issuing from the crater at the peak, while from several cracks along the side wreaths of steam arise. But at night it presents a grander and more awful spectacle.

The crescent moon reveals the pillar of smoke that continually belches from the mighty monster's bowels, and is not bright enough to dim the glowing patch of burning lava, which, like a huge figure seven turned the wrong way, quivers, and throbs and scintillates in the still night air. That glowing figure seven is a vast river of molten lava, more than a mile long, two hundred yards broad, and thirty feet deep, which was made by an eruption only a few months since. What a hint does it give us of the mighty pent-up forces, which once in a while break their bounds, just as they did two thousand years ago when Pompeii and Herculaneum slept peacefully, unsuspecting of evil, at the mountain's foot! You cannot see them; but there they lie, those buried, silent cities of the plain, such a contrast to the gay, noisy, brilliant Naples but half a score of miles away. There they have lain, under their cerements of lava and ashes, for nearly twenty centuries, and only one corner of the winding-sheet has yet been lifted.

As from Naples we look at the great mountain in the gloaming with the fiery gash glowing on its side, and think of the silent cities that lie buried above its pulsating heart, we can better understand than ever before why this destruction may have come. Naples to-day, as always, is full of all kinds of pimps and procurers, and lewd fellows of the baser sort. Silent witnesses unearthed at Pompeii show that she was far worse than modern Naples, and that her corruption was putrescent in its rottenness. Who will dare to say that there is no connection between God's fiery cinders and man's utter corruption?

Turn to the other side of the harbor, and you will see Puteoli, barely three miles distant, where Paul landed after his long and stormy journey about this time of year. He took "a ship of Alexandria" for Italy. To-morrow I expect to take a ship of Italy for Alexandria, over the same seas. May the humble disciple not have so long, boisterous, and adventurous a voyage as the great apostle.

XIV

THE OLDEST AND THE YOUNGEST;

Or, Christian Endeavor in the Land of the Pyramids

THE oldest civilization in the world and the youngest Christian organization in the world have met together; Egypt and Christian Endeavor have kissed each other, to adopt the Oriental imagery of this country.

Here, under the very eyes of the "far-seeing Sphinx," I find a Christian Endeavor welcome and the Christian Endeavor spirit.

At last "forty centuries look down" on this child of less than sixteen winters.

The foster-parent of Christian Endeavor in Egypt, who has, so to speak, acclimatized the Society in the land of the Pharaohs, is the Egyptian mission of the United Presbyterian Church of America. Some two years ago, the first society was started, and now there are three or four societies, including at least one Junior society at Asyoot, a long way up the Nile, where is one of the chief stations of the board. But especially to Dr. White and Miss Thompson of this mission should the thanks of all Christian Endeavorers be given for introducing the Society and watching over its interests.

I had but two days in Cairo altogether, but I had scarcely been there two hours when I was surprised and delighted to receive a visit from four Christian Endeavorers,—Dr. White and Rev. Mr. Reed of the mission, Rev. Mr. Lewis of America, and a young man from Cook's tourist office who is a stanch member of the Society, thus setting an example to many another young business man in a far land. They informed me that I was "billed" for an address the next night in the mission church under the auspices of "the Christian Endeavor society of Cairo."

This is the English-speaking society, and, as befits a cosmopolitan city like Cairo, where the ends of the earth come together, it is a very cosmopolitan society. Americans, English, Scotch, Irish, Welsh, Austrians, Egyptians, and I do not know how many other races, make up its membership. Its meetings are held Saturday afternoon, just before an English preaching-service, to which, of course, its members adjourn. The meetings are well attended, spirited, and spiritual.

On the night of the public meeting about a hundred and fifty came together, including the members of the Girls' Christian Endeavor Society of the mission. I was kindly introduced

A SHEIKH OF THE DESERT

by Dr. Harvey, one of the veteran missionaries of Egypt; and, as the whole audience understood English, I did not have to struggle with an interpreter, or an interpreter with me.

Let me congratulate the young people of the United Presbyterian Church of America on having such a splendid mission as the "mission in Egypt" to work for, pray for, and give to. In all the world around I do not know of another mission that has been more signally blessed of God. Practically it has the whole of Egypt for its field, as there is little done by any other society, and nobly has it seen and grasped its opportunity. It has 42 missionaries on the field, 401 native workers, more than 500 church members, more than 11,000 pupils gathered in 161 schools.

Moreover, the natives themselves are taught to give, as well as to pray and work, and Dr. Harvey told me that there were in the mission more than 400 Egyptian tithe givers. How is that for an example to Christian Endeavorers at home? I wonder whether the Tenth Legion of New York City will not admit these Egyptian brethren as affiliated members.

Well may the United Presbyterian Endeavorers feel a generous pride in this mission. May they hold in their memories and prayers the veterans, Dr. Watson and Dr. Harvey and Dr. Griffin and Dr. Murch of Cairo, as well as the many young missionaries, and also those in other parts of Egypt whom I did not meet; and by their prayers and their gifts may they support this work more and more generously.

XV

A UNIVERSITY WHERE "THE SUN DO MOVE"

THIS university is in Cairo, and it is the largest in the world. Harvard and Yale, Oxford and Cambridge, even Berlin and Halle, must yield the palm for numbers to the university of El Azhar in the land of the Pharaohs.

During a recent visit to Cairo I went through this university, accompanied by a newly arrived missionary, and with a fair Cairo Christian Endeavorer for guide.

Let me try to take my readers there to-day. We started from the substantial and commodious mission house of the United Presbyterian Board in an open carriage driven by a most irascible Arab "cabby."

While in the broader streets, where he had room enough to flourish and crack his whip to his heart's content, he uttered no expletives; but soon he turned into a narrow street in the native quarter, and then into a still narrower one with overhanging booths on each side, where the butcher and fez-maker, the barber and the potato-seller, were plying their trade in the broad glare of day. Then into a still narrower street he turned, where two people joining hands could touch the walls on each side.

A ragged camel with a huge bundle of brush fire-wood blocked our Jehu's way for a moment, and he cried out in classic Arabic, as he shook his fist at the offending camel-driver, "Get out of the way, you dog, you son of a dog, you grandson of a dog."

We looked to see the camel-driver square off at his antagonist in true Anglo-Saxon style. He did nothing of the sort, but simply hurled back some equally offensive epithets, and proceeded placidly on his way.

Then came a donkey-boy, athwart the road, the hair of his gray donkey beautifully tattooed with all sorts of geometrical figures. Our driver took special umbrage at the presumption of a donkey-boy in blocking his way, and cried out, "May your eyes be blasted, and may your mother go blind, and your grandmother, and all your relatives; out of the way, you pig." The donkey-boy gave him back as good as he sent, or as bad, rather; and after this vituperative fusillade was over we edged our way a few paces nearer the mosque for which we were bound. Such cries as these, many of them too vile for translation, are echoing all over the city of the caliphs, from dawn to dusk, from every alley and court.

At length our driver could go no further.

The narrow, filthy street became absolutely impassable, and we walked the few remaining yards to the university.

When I speak of a " university," dear reader, do not conjure up to yourself a Chicago or a Princeton, with vast buildings, extensive dormitories, Gothic chapels, and the like. Neither are there here orderly classrooms, desks, or forms, or any of the paraphernalia of a university to which we are accustomed.

The first demand made upon us, as we stepped within the carved portal, was to take off our shoes; or, if we would not do that, to put on a pair of huge felt slippers, in which we went skating and sliding over the slippery mats.

As we entered the doorway, a number of the students came rushing out, some little fellows not more than a dozen years old (for the full course occupies eight or ten years, and they will be full-grown men before they are through), others already well on toward middle age. The majority, however, seemed to be eighteen or twenty years old, about the age of our college boys at home.

Entering the next room of the mosque, we were fairly in the midst of them, in the most literal sense of the term, for they were squatted on the floor in little groups, each numbering from six to thirty, and it was with difficulty that we avoided treading on some outstretched figure. Many of them were studying aloud in a singsong, nasal tone, swaying their bodies back and forth with a rhythmical swing, in order to give proper elasticity to their minds.

What a Babel it made! A thousand students in this one hall, perhaps, each one of them apparently trying to outshout his neighbor, in his eagerness to beat some knotty portion of the Koran into his own unwilling brain.

Many of the groups, however, had a professor in the midst, who sat cross-legged on a little raised dais, while the students squatted around him on every side. Bright and intelligent men were many of these professors. They seemed to be asking questions, to which the students would shout the answers at the top of their voices, each eager to get ahead of his companions in vociferation. Some of the teachers, however, were evidently giving lectures, while the students took copious notes.

As we entered one hall of the mosque, where an unusually large circle of boys was gathered around a professor, our ears were greeted by an unmistakable hiss; and then another took it up, and another, until all in the room were giving vent to the same sibilant reproach, and it seemed as if a thousand geese were craning their necks for a long, strong hiss-s-s-s.

I have frequently heard vigorous demonstrations of another sort from Christian Endeavor audiences in different lands, but it was my first experience of such vigorous expressions of disapproval. Not being aware of having committed any offence worthy of such emphatic condemnation, I asked my fair guide what it all meant. She said we were taken for English people, and that the university students bore a grudge against us, because the English authorities, on the appearance of the cholera and the finding of some dead bodies within the university, had insisted, most wisely, on some sanitary measures, on the cleansing of the Augean stable, and the closing of some portions of the university. Our ruffled feelings were soothed by this explanation, since we felt that, like so many better men before us, we were hissed in a good cause.

So we passed on through room after room of this vast mosque. In every one was the same sort of groups of red-fezzed, squatting figures, boisterously conning their books.

What is studied in this strange university, do you ask? The question can be answered in two words,—" The Koran." To be sure, the Arabic language, grammar, rhetoric, logic, and even jurisprudence, all have their place here, but only that the Koran may be understood more completely. Everything for the Mohammedan centres around this book, which has so mightily affected the destiny of millions of our fellow mortals.

In the schools of lower grade, too, the Koran is the one object of study. The boy, after learning to read, learns the first chapter by heart, and then the last, and then the last but one, and so on in reverse order. "Although the language is often difficult and obscure, no explanations are given, so that the boy who knows the whole book by heart usually understands but little of it. As soon as the boy has learned the whole of the Koran, his education is finished; and the completion of his studies is commemorated by the celebration of the Khatnich, a family festival, to which the schoolmaster is invited."

Even in the highest university of all, which I have described, no science, no natural history, no mathematics, is studied. "The sun do move," is still the belief of the devout Mussulman. For aught I know, he still thinks the earth rests on a huge turtle, with a vast canopy of brass overhead. The power of electricity is still conjurer's magic to him, and the Koran is the beginning and end of his education.

After all, in spite of this superstition, ignorance, and density, is there not a lesson here for Western Christians? The faith of Islam is still a mighty factor in the world to be reckoned with. It rules the lives of untold millions. A Mohammedan convert to Christianity is the rarest of converts. Why? Because he knows his sacred book. It is all in all to him. How may we make more steadfast, faithful Christians? Let us take a leaf from the history of the Moslem; study our sacred Book as he studies the false prophet. Our Bible will not displace or dispute true science, but it alone will make stalwart Christians.

XVI

CONCERNING MANY THINGS ON SEA AND SHORE

I AM writing at Ahmednuggur, in western India; and, as I write, the firing of big guns, and the rattle of musketry, and the blare of brass bands from the British parade-ground, remind me that it is the first day of the year, while the hideous din of a Hindu wedding that is taking place under my window forcibly tells me that I am in a heathen land.

But through the open window with the early morning light comes the sweet, cool air of an Indian winter's morning, a morning like our rarest days in June, reminding me that, whatever the din of war or of heathenism, the atmosphere of God still envelops this old world.

> "God's in his heaven;
> All's right with the world."

After leaving the Christian Endeavorers of Cairo we steamed through the Suez Canal, and down the hot Red Sea for five days, and then across the Indian Ocean for five days more, in the teeth of a strong northeast monsoon, which somewhat delayed our good ship.

I use the plural "we" with the understanding that you are all taking the journey with me, though as a matter of fact it is only the singular and melancholy "I" that embarked, and one ticket answers for us all. The travelling companion of many voyages could not go with me on this long journey; so that in my loneliness I make the more of your imaginary companionship. However, there were on the Valetta no less than ten Christian Endeavorers, (where will you not find Christian Endeavorers in these days?) and we had a delightful meeting on the Sunday evening of our voyage on the Red Sea.

Two of the Endeavorers were from Illinois, one from Ohio, one from Missouri, two from Canada, two from Australia, one from Massachusetts, and one from England,—a cosmopolitan Endeavor meeting, you see. Several were coming as missionaries to India and Ceylon.

Sunday noon, December 27, in the broiling heat of Indian midday we landed at Bombay. Sad indeed is the condition of this great city, the second city in population in the British Empire. One hundred cases a day of bubonic plague (the old Black Death that depopulated London in the seventeenth century); nearly as many deaths; little disinfecting fires burning on the sidewalk before many of the houses, showing that death is within; the burning ghats blazing night and day; one hundred bodies waiting for cremation at a single crematory; people fleeing from the city by the ten thousand by every railway;—such, in a sentence, is the story of the great plague of 1896-97.

These words have acquired a new significance to me of late: "There shall no evil befall thee, neither shall any plague come nigh thy dwelling."

Three hours after landing I preached in the beautiful Scotch church; and a little later the same evening I spoke to the Endeavorers of the American mission church. Connected with this church are really five societies: one general society for the church, and four Junior societies for the boys and girls of the schools. All flourish under the kindly care of Mr. and Mrs. Hume.

On account of the plague the public Christian Endeavor meetings which had been planned had to be given up, as the physicians advised against all general gatherings, and my stay in Bombay was shortened to less than two days.

From Bombay to Poonah is a single night's ride by train, and here I was the guest of Mr. Robert Wilder, whom many of you remember with great affection for the missionary inspiration he brought to many of our early conventions. He is doing a magnificent work for the students of India.

A BURNING GHAT

The address was given in the Soldiers' Home of Poonah, under the auspices of the Poonah Christian Endeavor society, of which Mr. Reed, the earnest chaplain of the post, is the president.

After the address two red-coated soldiers lingered to talk about their souls' salvation with Dr. Grattan Guinness, who was also present.

It was a most affecting scene. We all knelt down on the floor, half a dozen soldiers, Dr. Guinness, Mr. Wilder, Mr. Reed, and myself. Some earnest prayers were offered for the two wavering ones. They were urged to commit themselves to Christ. At length, after a long pause, one of them began to sing upon his knees, with bowed head and in a trembling voice:

> "Lord Jesus, I long to be perfectly whole;
> I want thee forever to dwell in my soul;
> Break down every idol, cast out every foe;
> Now wash me, and I shall be whiter than snow."

Then the other soldier offered a broken, earnest prayer, and both rose from their knees, saved men, I trust. Mr. McBain, a noble officer, "the father of his regiment," on whose breast gleams more than one medal won in battle for his country, is the secretary of this society.

XVII

A PLAGUE-STRICKEN CITY

It is difficult for people who have not seen the plague face to face, to realize that the horrors of the scourge of the Middle Ages are possible in this year of our Lord.

Where are our doctors? what are our sanitary engineers doing? what has become of the plumber, with his traps and drains and cut-offs and lengthy bills,—that all these guardians of the public health should allow so terrible an outbreak of violent disease to half depopulate one of the greatest cities of the world, and spread possible contagion to the four quarters of the globe?

People looked for such periodical outbreaks in the sixteenth and seventeenth centuries, but we pityingly and patronizingly speak of those days as the "dark ages" of sanitary science, when plumbers were an unknown quantity, and medicine was but little removed from the powdered snails and pellets of medicated frogs' eyes which the doctors of China affect to-day.

But this is the nineteenth century, and its waning half-decade at that; this is the age of lymphs and serum and microbe-destroyers and bacteria-fighters; this is the age of Jenner and Pasteur and Koch; and yet, in the presence of such a pestilence as that from which Bombay is suffering, the doctors are at their wits' end, and we might apparently as well be back in the century of Daniel Defoe.

Bombay is the second city in size in the British Empire. Its nearly one million of inhabitants places it before Glasgow, Liverpool, Manchester, and Melbourne, and next to London itself in population. Moreover, it is a city not only great in size, but great in commercial importance, in influence and enterprise. It is the "Eye of India." Some of the most imposing buildings in the world are found here. The Victoria Railway Station, for instance, is probably the most magnificent building of its kind on the planet. Euston, St. Pancras, the great station at Frankfort-on-the-Main, the Grand Central on Forty-Second Street, and even the splendid Union Terminal at St. Louis, must hide their diminished heads before this queen of railway stations, the Victoria.

So also the university, the post-office, the great hospitals, and the new municipal buildings can hold their own when compared with those of any European or American city.

Moreover, Bombay is probably one of the most picturesque as well as one of the most cosmopolitan cities on the face of the globe.

The European and the Asiatic, the ruling nation and the subject races, "plain" and colored, black and white, and all the shades of tan and brown, jostle one another in the streets of Bombay as in no other city in the world.

Here, in a short walk of a quarter of a mile, you see the dignified Moslem with his long puggaree (just the length of his final winding sheet) wound around his head into a most becoming turban. You see the mild-eyed, handsome, high-caste Brahman with his orange-and-gold topc. You see the rich Parsee in his high glazed hat, surpassed in ugliness only by the Englishman's "stovepipe." You see the modern belle in tailor-made gown just out from Worth's, and, side by side with her on the street, a Parsee lady, clad in graceful garments of costly silk, a single length swathing her in its ample folds from head to heels.

You will see little Lord Fauntleroy with fair flaxen curls and pallid cheeks, showing that he must soon go back to England to escape the dreaded Indian climate so fatal to children, and, not ten feet away, a little Indian lad and lass, *sans* hat, *sans* shoes, *sans* trousers or jacket or dress, as bare as they came from their Maker, —naked and not ashamed.

Said a friend of mine to me the other day, and I believe the statement is true, "No one could get himself up in a costume so bizarre or fantastic as to cause an old resident of Bombay to turn his head or take even a languid interest in the passer-by."

If a man should appear in Bombay with a frying-pan on his head for a hat, a big string of beads on his manly breast in lieu of a coat, a barrel-hoop dependent from each ear, a small crowbar stuck through his nose, one hip swathed in red calico and the other as nature made it, with a pair of forty-league boots on his feet,—if, in this costume, he should parade the streets of Bombay, he would not be locked up in a lunatic asylum. By no means! He would be considered one of "our highly esteemed fellow-citizens." No small boy would follow him with derisive hoots; no reporter would interview him for an extra edition; in fact, no one would look at him twice.

In such a city, so diverse in its characteristics, so cosmopolitan in its population, has the bubonic plague broken out. It is the same fell pestilence that depopulated London. As 1666 is known as the year of the great plague in London, so 1897 will be known as the great plague year of Bombay.

I reached Bombay on the 27th of December, 1896, when the plague was assuming its worst type and when the number of deaths each day was extremely large.

The view of the city as one enters the beautiful harbor is charming in the extreme. After five days on the Indian Ocean with nothing but the scudding schools of flying-fish to break the monotony of the voyage, and five days previously on the Red Sea, where the occasional glimpses of land are terrifically stern and forbidding, one is well prepared for the palm-clad shores, and for a beautiful modern city of substantial business blocks, whose streets are lined with noble, spreading banyan-trees.

From a distance it looks like anything but a plague-stricken city, it must be confessed. Life and not death seems to have its home here. But one cannot be long on shore without feeling the depression of a place over which the angel of destruction is hovering. Everywhere I saw evidences of his presence. The closed shops, the half-deserted streets, the absence of wedding and festive processions, which usually at this time of year make Bombay a perfect kaleidoscope of life and color, all proclaim that something is wrong.

But there are more tangible signs of pestilence. Here is a hovel from whose roof all the tiles have been torn off to let in the blessed, purifying sunlight upon some dark, disease-breeding hole. In front of a dozen houses in the next street through which we pass are little disinfecting fires burning, showing that the plague has come near that dwelling and perhaps claimed half its occupants for its own. Hundreds of these little sidewalk fires are burning all over the city, pointing out the infected houses to the passer-by. They are built of short sticks of hard wood, on which is sprinkled an abundant supply of sulphur. Of what value this can be, only the city fathers of Bombay know. The fumes cannot reach the houses with any degree of effectiveness, and, though they may disinfect the air to a slight degree and thus benefit the passing traveller, the benefit must be nearly infinitesimal.

But other and more effective means are employed. Whenever an infected house is discovered it is visited by a squad of municipal officers; the furniture is cleared out, the bedding is burned, and the interior is thoroughly whitewashed. In many cases, too, the tiles are torn off the roof to let in the purifying sun.

One of the most effective measures yet devised is the cutting off of the water-supply from the poorer houses of the infected district. In the dark and noisome passageways where hundreds of thousands of these people live, in abodes little bigger than underground drains, the free supply of city water has been a bane rather than a boon. The taps were always running or dripping, and earthen floors were always damp and soaked with filth, forming a very hotbed for disease. Of course the people objected to the cutting off of their water-supply, and deep and loud were the grunts and growls against this interference with their rights, even though they had only to go out into the street to draw water from the ever-flowing pipes. But the authorities persisted, and this fruitful source of disease has been removed.

Another plan, tried to a larger extent, and to a degree successful, is the segregation of plague-stricken households. But there is fierce and bitter opposition on the part of many of the natives to the idea of segregation. All sorts of stories are rife among them as to the object of the authorities. Some even think that their hearts will be plucked out and made into charms by which the foreign doctors hope to conjure away the plague.

Another scheme has been proposed, but as yet has found very little favor: it is to draw a cordon around the infected city, to station troops all along the line, and to allow no one from Bombay to go beyond this boundary. It is argued, and with a great deal of reason, that this would only intensify the pestilence in the spots already infected, would create an uncontrollable panic among those who could not get away, and would almost doom the city to destruction.

The causes to which the more ignorant of the population ascribe the plague are various; in fact, almost every cause except the right one, the filth and unsanitary condition of their city, is assigned. Some ascribe it to the malevolence of their deities, and others to the unfortunate conjunction of the stars, while still others, most curiously, have laid the burden upon the aged shoulders of Queen Victoria. A few months ago her beautiful Jubilee statue was defaced by some miscreants with a liberal coating of tar. This outrage was deplored by all well-meaning people, and was denounced in the native as well as in the English papers. But many of the people believe that the apologies rendered at the time were not sufficient, and that now the old queen is visiting her wrath upon the city that defiled her image.

A friend of mine engaged in zenana work was refused admission one day by some of the women who before had always heartily welcomed her. When she came to learn the cause, she found that it was because she was supposed to be a spy of the English government in the service of the queen, who had come to ferret out the misdemeanors of the people and to punish with the plague any murmuring against her gentle sway.

It can readily be imagined that business is suffering terribly and that many industries are almost at a standstill. Master-workmen cannot induce laborers to enter their employ. Clothing-houses and shoemakers' shops are deserted by the workmen. Many factories have had to close their doors, and in every branch of life the effect of the pestilence is felt. The government has been compelled to issue very stringent orders concerning the civil servants, threatening them with expulsion and with loss of pension if they yield to the prevailing panic and leave the city. One of the results of the plague is strange indeed. Litigation has come almost to a standstill. Case after case is called, we are told, only to disclose the fact that parties or witnesses are not forthcoming. It would appear that the judges are sitting rather for the sake of setting an example than for the sake of the work they can get through. But unless matters mend, says *The Pioneer*, they will absolutely be at the end of their business and the sitting will be closed by the force of circumstances.

In spite of all efforts and precautions, the plague has increased in the number of its victims and in the mortality of those attacked, and the authorities seem utterly unable to cope with the destroyer. Medical science is baffled, and sanitary experts appear to be of little avail.

It is not to be wondered at that all sorts of quacks and nostrum-venders should come to the fore at such a time as this, and many of the remedies are of an unearthly and immaterial sort. Fakirs promise that if due reverence is paid to the divinities they worship, the plague will soon disappear, and grave announcements to this effect are frequently made in the daily papers. Not only the native papers but the English journals contain many strange announcements in these days. Here is one copied *verbatim* from the leading Bombay daily, printed therein without comment or reflection of any kind:—

"Pandit Swaroopdas telegraphs to us from Shikarpore: I undertake to free Bombay of its plague, if goat-flesh, fish, and liquor are supplied to me for sacrificial purposes in quantities sufficient to equal, approximately, a day's consumption in Bombay. Further condition is that no slaughter of larger animals should take place on the day the sacrifice is offered. I am ready to leave for Bombay on invitation. I require neither remuneration nor travelling expenses."

Many other proposals to pacify the enraged deities have been published, but, so far as I know, the city authorities have not seen fit to adopt these means to secure immunity from the plague.

It can be well imagined that the signs of death are numerous in every direction. On the day of my arrival in Bombay no less than ten funerals passed the house of the friend with whom I was staying, and it was mournful in the extreme to hear the wails of the afflicted, and the still more dreadful noises of the native musicians who often accompany a funeral train. Sometimes these processions bear the poor body to its last resting-place in the middle of the night, and it is weird and melancholy in the last degree to awake at two o'clock in the morning, perhaps, to the horrid din of a funeral procession, and to hear the monotonous refrain of the bearers, " Ram, Ram, Sachha ! " (" Ram is true ! ") repeated over and over and over again.

If a Mohammedan is being borne to his last resting-place, the unchanging cry of the mourners and the bearers is, " There is one God, and Mohammed is his prophet."

Busy indeed are these days at the various burning-ghats of the city. As we drove, one evening, on one of the principal streets behind a high wall we could see a brilliant flame shooting upward and illumining the sky above and the blank wall beyond. This was one of the burning-ghats where the Hindu dead are cremated, and, looking through the open doorway, we could see scores of lurid fires licking up the bodies placed between the glowing logs. The sticks of wood which are used for cremation purposes are about six feet long. Of these a platform is built some four feet broad and two feet high. Upon this platform the dead body is placed; other logs are piled upon it; and pieces of sandal-wood and other fragrant woods are added to the pile. Sacred passages from holy books are read by the officiating priests; the nearest relative then walks three times round the funeral pile, and applies the torch, and in about two hours nothing but a handful of ashes tells of the father or mother or child that was borne within the ghat. More than a hundred bodies, I was assured, were waiting for cremation at one of these burning-ghats in a single day.

The vultures, too, in Bombay are particularly busy during this dreadful epidemic. As is well known, the Parsees are a numerous and influential sect in Bombay. They are sometimes called "the Yankees of the Orient," because of their ability to get on in the world. They neither bury their dead nor burn them, since both fire and earth are sacred to their religion. So they give them to the vultures by exposing them on the Towers of Silence. It is a most grewsome and melancholy spectacle to see these horrid birds of prey awaiting their victims. The towers, large structures of stone and cement, are on Malabar Hill, one of the most beautiful parts of Bombay, and are approached by winding roads through lovely gardens.

These towers are about ninety feet in diameter and fifteen or twenty feet high. On the edge of the towers, often sitting as closely together as they can be packed, are the vultures, waiting with horrid impatience for the next victim that shall be given to their ravenous beaks and claws. Up the long winding road come the mourners, chanting funeral prayers; then follows a man leading a white dog, the emblem of faithfulness; then come a number of priests and the relatives of the family, two and two, holding a white handkerchief between them, which indicates that a bond of sympathy draws them together. When they reach the house of prayer, the mourners enter and engage in prayer while the corpse is borne into the Tower of Silence. The body is exposed naked on a platform erected on the inside, which cannot be seen by spectators without. The moment the bearers withdraw, the hungry vultures swoop down upon the corpse, and in ten minutes nothing but the skeleton remains, picked clean of every particle of flesh. For two or three weeks the skeleton is allowed to remain there, when it is thrown into a common pit beneath, with tens of thousands of its nameless companions. Some of these are of high degree, and some of low, but death, the great Leveller, makes no distinction in the Parsee Tower of Silence.

The following grim paragraph concerning the vultures and their dreadful business I have just cut from a Bombay paper. It shows as nothing else can do how soon people will get used to the direst calamities and the most grewsome details, so that they become a matter of commonplace and every-day comment.

"On inquiries regarding vultures and their ability to consume the twelve or thirteen bodies of Parsees taken on an average to the Towers of Silence daily, the Secretary to the Parsee Panchayet has informed the representative of a Bombay paper that the number of vultures has considerably increased of late, and that there is not any truth in the statement that bodies remain unconsumed and are thrown over in the big pit in the middle of the Towers. The fact was, he stated, that in ordinary times the flock of vultures did not subsist on the three or four bodies that were brought in, but soared away to their chief roosting-place and gorged on animal and other food obtainable there. Now they have, by instinct, flocked to the Towers of Silence, and no complaint about their being slack in the work of despatching the dead bodies has been made."

One of the most pathetic sights during these terrible days in Bombay is that of the thousands of poor people who are attempting to flee the city. On the day I left Bombay by the Great Indian Peninsula Route, twelve thousand people, by two lines of road alone, had joined the panic-stricken exodus. The railway stations and all the streets and open spaces in the vicinity were crowded with squatting figures in white cloths, waiting for a chance to board a third-class railway compartment and thus leave the infected precincts.

Huddled together in all sorts of heaps of humanity, in the dead of night as well as in the broad glare of day, were these waiting, frightened throngs. The trains were running in two sections, and all the third-class compartments were crowded to suffocation. Thousands of others left by sea or by the carriage roads, and already it is thought that nearly half the population has shaken the dust of Bombay from its feet and turned its face countryward. The exodus is estimated all the way from two hundred thousand to four hundred thousand, and probably the latter number is more nearly correct. Not all those who try to escape reach the promised land safely, for almost every day, it is said, some corpses are taken out of the trains, and others live only long enough to reach Poonah or Ahmednuggur or some other port of hoped-for safety, and there yield to the destroyer whose seeds of death have been implanted in their systems.

Altogether, the sight of a plague-stricken city is sad beyond expression, and the sympathy of the civilized world has not been expended in vain upon the "Eye of India," so sadly and grievously afflicted.

XVIII

CONCERNING A DELIGHTFUL EXPERIENCE

To-day, my fellow travellers, let us go to Sirur on a personally conducted visit to the Endeavorers of this enterprising mission station.

Sirur, you must know, is a station of the American Board in the Mahratta country, about one hundred and fifty miles from Bombay. We go to Poonah by rail, and there we must take a tonga, drawn by tough little Deccan horses, for Sirur, forty-one miles away. We start before daylight to avoid the dreadful heat of midday.

Our tonga wallah unmercifully whips up his raw-boned little nags, starved by the famine like many another animal, four-footed and two-footed. As we do not know the Mahrati word for "stop," all our expostulations are in vain.

It is a most fascinating ride of forty-one miles in the cool of the lovely Indian winter morning; past queer little villages of mud and straw, swarming with human life; past grotesque Hindu temples filled with hideous obscene gods; under spreading banyan-trees, whose branches are musical with birds of gorgeous plumage.

But I have not time to describe the ride, for I want to introduce you at once to your fellow Endeavorers. Here they are drawn up before the mission bungalow of Sirur, which we reach before noon. The girls are in bright red cloths or graceful white tunics trimmed with red, the boys in nondescript garments, but all clothed in some way, and thus showing at first glance their difference from the heathen children, who are clad chiefly in an expansive smile.

Two great banyan-trees were festooned and arched over with bunting, thus forming a sort of triumphal arch in our honor, while several Christian Endeavor banners and a hearty Christian Endeavor song as we drove up completed the welcome.

Mr. and Mrs. Winsor, the missionaries in charge, awaited us on the shady veranda of the bungalow, and at once made us feel that we were at home.

After the dust of travel had been disposed of, and breakfast as well, for breakfast in this sunny land comes anywhere between nine and noon, we visited the excellent boys' school, where some capital drawings were displayed; and the girls' school, where the pretty black-eyed damsels recited with great spirit a dialogue for our benefit, and went through some excellent calisthenic exercises. Then we went to the pleasant mission church, which was crowded to the doors with Christians, while half-naked heathen Hindus thronged the doors and windows.

Some of the non-Christians too, were not afraid to come within the doors; among them, the Mussulman chief of the whole district, who told me afterward that he rejoiced that I had come, that "we all worship the same God," etc., while he emphasized his friendliness by sending a present of fruit and cake to the mission bungalow. Evidently Mohammedanism is a different thing under British rule in India from what it is in bloody Turkey. Here its talons are clipped and its beak is broken.

Most hearty was the welcome that was given to Christian Endeavor at this meeting. We were sung to, and spoken at, and garlanded, and rubbed with rose-water. According to the beautiful Mahratta custom, a heavy garland of beautiful white flowers like tuberoses was hung around our necks, a wristlet of flowers was put upon each wrist, a few drops of the precious attar of roses were rubbed on the back of each hand, and a green leaf containing the famous betelnut was given us to chew. Then an address was made by "Dr. Clark Sahib," and translated by Mr. Winsor. The climax of the service of welcome was reached, when a beautiful orange-red, high-caste Brahman's hat was presented to your representative by the pastor of the church. In a flowery and poetic speech, he in effect said that every casket should have a cover, and, as the hat was the cover to the brain, they gave me this Brahman's tile, that I might keep within my brain pleasant impressions of the visit to Sirur.

Then the formal meeting was over, and we shook hands and "salaamed" in the most profuse and Oriental style. After this, four mothers with their little new babies came up asking that "Clark Sahib" would give them names. What could I do but comply with this gracious request? Here are the names that they will bear :—

HARRIET CLARK LASHMIYA NAGAYA.
MAUDE WILLISTON HANAMANT ZOTEBA.
EDWARD LAXAMAN DAMAJI.
JOHN WILLIS ANANDRA LIMBAJI.

Afterward another mother asked me to name her little boy. What better could I do than call him

WILLIAM SHAW MADAWAROW AMOLIK?

I gave each of the babies a Junior Christian Endeavor badge, and the mothers and fathers seemed much delighted with the names.

Some of these mothers have most interesting histories. Maude Williston Hanamant's mother, for instance, was sold by her grandfather to the authorities of the temple of the most obscene god, to be brought up in all the nameless horrors of a Nautch girl's life. With great difficulty she was rescued by the missionaries; she has grown up to be a beautiful, pure Christian woman, and is now the wife of one of the most honored teachers in the mission schools.

I know a little six-year-old boy who sometimes prays, "Dear Jesus, bless dear grandpa and grandma, and help them to grow up to be good men and women." I can only pray that these babies may "grow up to be good men and women," and good Christian Endeavorers like their namesakes.

I have described this meeting somewhat at length, because in its heartiness it is typical of many another welcome. I can but mention the splendid Industrial School in Sirur, in which work Mrs. Winsor is a pioneer, and the pleasant days at Ahmednuggur, an old and strong station of the American Board, the centre of a score of Christian Endeavor societies, where at meeting after meeting the large church was thronged with intelligent Christians.

XIX

A QUEER HOSPITAL

The abundance of animal life in India is one of the things which first of all strikes the traveller. Wherever he goes, birds and beasts seem to swarm in numbers never approached in western climes. He sees not simply a few impertinent English sparrows, whose numbers can never be diminished, even by the small boy with his gun; not simply a timid and far-sighted crow here and there, which smells the hunter's gun a mile away; but such a variety and quantity of living creatures as arouse the untamed hunter's instinct at every turn.

Bright green parrots alight on the telegraph wires; herds of spotted deer scamper off into the jungle as the train approaches, or perhaps, made bold by constant familiarity, they do not even lift their cottony tails and run, but graze quietly beside the railway track. Wild peacocks with extended tails, on every feather a brilliant painted eye, stalk lazily over the stubble fields as the train whizzes past. Monkeys chatter in the branches of the banyan-trees, and perform acrobatic feats for the amusement of the passer-by.

The great reason, I suppose, for the superabundance of animal life in India is that the country is largely inhabited by vegetarians. The great majority of the people in India, after centuries of training, have come to regard the eating of meat with horror and disgust; and the lusty beef-eaters who live in the land of John Bull or Brother Jonathan are regarded by many of the mild-eyed Hindus with a peculiar loathing.

One result of this reverence for animal life has been the establishment in all the large cities of India of hospitals for aged and infirm animals. Here the lame, halt, and blind of the animal kingdom are gathered together. Raw-boned oxen that have been overworked and half starved are here tenderly cared for until they die.

Spavined and wind-galled horses are here collected from their cruel owners. Mangy dogs and half-starved Thomas cats; animals big and little, wild and tame, here form a happy family in the strangest menagerie that was ever seen. These queer hospitals are often very largely endowed by rich Hindus, who are supposed thus to please their benign deities and gain an easy entrance into heaven.

It is even said that some of the stricter Hindus carry their reverence for animal life so far that they will not disturb a mosquito at his evening meal, or interfere with certain creatures, not mentioned in polite society or numbered in the census, when they are foraging for their daily blood pudding.

It is gravely asserted that in one city a man is hired for a small salary to furnish meat and drink for the fleas that are turned loose upon him, and that he not only earns his daily bread in this way, but cultivates the grace of patience at the same time.

This regard for animals, many of which are supposed to be incarnations of some special deity, is particularly shown at some of the famous temples of India. For instance, when on a recent Christian Endeavor pilgrimage to Benares, I visited in the intervals between the meetings the famous Monkey Temple. Swarms of little grinning parodies of men surrounded me as soon as I set foot within the sacred precincts. Some large apes, aged and sedate, would ask in a dignified way for the cakes and parched corn which every visitor is supposed to bring them. But at the same time a score of little fellows, younger and less dignified, would jump down upon their aged relatives and filch the tidbits out from under their very eyes.

The precincts of this temple, with its hideous goddess grinning behind a screen within the holy of holies, also swarmed with other kinds of animals, gathering for the sake of receiving the crumbs that fell from the monkeys' tables. Black and white goats nosed about with a confidential air of familiarity. Mongrel curs dogged our heels. Gray and black ravens perched upon the haunches of the goats, that they might get their share of good things; and altogether it was a zoölogical garden of tame animals such as I never saw before.

"What the monkeys are to Vishnu, the sacred zebu is to Siva," we are told; "and so the cow and bull are the objects of special worship to the Hindus; their slaughter is a terrible crime, and to eat their flesh is loss of caste in this world and far worse in the world to come. It is a most meritorious act to dedicate bulls and cows to Siva, and to multiply around the god the living images of Nandi, the divine steed. These animals are always numerous in places sacred to this god, where they live in perfect freedom, pampered and fed by pious devotees, who tempt their appetites with dainties put out on the doorstep in a pot, and let them wander unchecked into any shop they fancy, to help themselves to any grain or vegetables for which their souls may lust."

In contrast to this care and regard for animal life on the part of the heathen Hindu, the cruelty of the brutal Anglo-Saxon is sometimes brought out in hideous contrast. For instance, on a recent journey through Central India, there were on the same train with myself some private soldiers, who were taking the same long journey of twenty-four hours. For a time they beguiled the tedium of the way by coaxing to their compartment in the train every poor, mangy dog which they could induce to come near them with a chicken-bone or a piece of bread. Then, when the dog got within striking distance, with a heavy hockey stick they would hit him with all their might over the back or legs. I saw them break the back of one poor dog and the leg of another that went off crying with a most pitiable "ki-i-i." By this time I thought it was time to interfere, and, as few people travel in this part of India except government officials and military officers, I knew that "Tommy Atkins" would take me for one of his superior officers. So, putting my head into the compartment where the four human brutes were seated, I said to them: "You are the most cruel and cowardly men I've ever seen in my life, to beat the poor dogs in this way. If I know of your doing anything more of this sort on this journey, I will report you to the general in command at Agra." It is needless to say that these particular "Tommies" were cowardly as well as brutal. They said not a word, but slunk into a corner of the compartment, and I heard no more yelping dogs that day.

In the same compartment with me on that journey were some high-caste Brahmans, who were equally indignant with myself over this wanton cruelty, though they did not dare to say anything to its perpetrators. I said to myself, as they were groaning in sympathy with the wounded dogs, "What will these gentle heathen think of our vaunted Christianity, when, after nineteen centuries, we must admit that such human brutes still exist?" Such are the men that make missionary work in India mountainously difficult.

It must be admitted, however, that there is an enormous amount of cruelty in this land of the Orient. To be sure, the Hindus will not take animal life, but in many cases it would be much more merciful if they would do so. They will let a poor dog with broken bones and covered with sores drag out a miserable existence rather than put him out of misery. They will starve their horses and underfeed their cattle for the sake of the few annas which they thus save. They will twist the tails of their bullocks by way of urging them to greater speed, until the caudal extremities of the poor animals are broken in a dozen places. They will leave a poor, famished creature by the roadside to die of slow starvation rather than by the swift bullet or the merciful knife. A few of these creatures, to be sure, find their way into the animal hospital, but only a few comparatively, and for the most part the animals of Christian countries are as much better off as are the human beings.

The religion of Christ has brought health and happiness, not only to the human race, but to the domestic animals of Christian lands as well. Then " praise ye Him," not only " kings of the earth and all people," " young men and maidens, old men and children," but " beasts and all cattle, creeping things and flying fowl," " let *them* praise the name of the Lord."

XX

HERE AND THERE IN INDIA

From Sirur we went to Ahmednuggur. Here are two churches and a very large Christian community. Four meetings were held, each one crowded with native Christians. Thence we went on to Harda in the Central Provinces, a twelve hours' ride from "Nagar."

A half-dozen missionaries were on the platform to greet us, and I should think nearly a hundred Endeavorers were drawn up in two lines, on both sides of the road, just outside of the station compound.

They carried, on long poles, beautiful silk banners, with "Christian Endeavor" and our Endeavor mottoes in Hindi characters embroidered thereon. As Mr. Wharton, the senior missionary of the station, and I passed through this line, they chanted their welcome, until we mounted the "garry," and the little white bullocks, with humps on their shoulders, trotted us off to the mission bungalow. Altogether the two days in Harda were most delightful and encouraging. The true spirit of Christian Endeavor enthusiasm and fellowship prevailed.

Harda is a mission station of the Disciples of

Christ of the United States; but not only did the workers of this mission come together from different stations, but the Friends of England, who have stations near by, united with them. One of the Friends, Samuel Baker, a most accomplished Hindi scholar, interpreted for me at all the sessions. I assure you we did not waste any time. Saturday evening as soon as the dust of travel was washed off, and Sunday morning before breakfast, and Sunday afternoon, and Sunday evening, we came together. Which meeting of all was the most *delightful*, it would be hard to say.

Perhaps the most *important* was the little parlor gathering of missionaries and workers on the last evening, when the Christians-Friend or Friends-Christian local union was organized for Harda and vicinity. "Vicinity" is a very large word hereabout, and what this union as yet lacks in number of societies it makes up in extent of territory, for it covers a small empire.

Never have I seen more earnest missionaries, more intelligent appreciation of the claims of Christian Endeavor, or greater harmony and brotherhood than in these two missions.

Let me congratulate the young Christians of America and the young Friends of England on the privilege they have of supporting so promising a work.

Rutlam, distant a night's ride by rail in Central India, the capital of the native state of Rutlam, was our next stopping-place. This station and others near by are under the charge of the Canadian Presbyterian Church, and a fruitful and hopeful mission it is.

My kind hosts were Mr. and Mrs. Campbell, and a dozen other missionaries of the same mission came together for the conference. Here is a good native society, and the promise, I believe, of many more.

After Rutlam our zigzag journey took us to Ajmeer, a British town surrounded by Rajputana states.

Here is an English society recruited from the Methodist and Scotch missions, and embracing some residents and soldiers; and I hope before long to hear of many good native societies in the Scotch mission churches, which are strong in all this region.

There are some native Epworth Leagues in this vicinity; but they do not unite with us in our Christian Endeavor services, I am sorry to say.

While in Ajmeer, the guest of the kindest of hosts, Mr. and Mrs. De Souza, I met Miss Mary Murray, one of the three Murray sisters, formerly of Switzerland, but now of India, but always and everywhere of Christian Endeavor.

This, I feel, is but a dry and meagre account of a week's wanderings, during which I have usually travelled all night and spoken two or three times every day,—a busy life, you see, which does not give me much time for chatting on paper with you or any other friends.

How I wish I had time and room to put in some graphic touches to tell of the picturesque scenes that make this hard journey one of unflagging interest!

I would tell you, for instance, of the wretched beggars, made by the awful famine now raging in India; of the hundreds of skinny hands stretched out for a handful of corn by hungry mortals along the roadside, sometimes huddled together as thick as they can squat.

I would tell you of the interesting leper asylum in Harda; of the old leper who rode by my side in the railway car for fifty miles, and hid his disease, which had eaten off most of his fingers, under the euphemism of "skin disease." Skin disease, indeed!

I would tell you of the gorgeous "durbar" or reception given by the rajah of Rutlam on the occasion of his seventeenth birthday, to which I was invited, and of the call I received next day from the Parsee regent and governor of Rutlam, and how I went off to the station behind the prancing chargers of "His Royal Highness," the rajah, attended by a military escort on white horses. Do not think, however, that your correspondent will be unduly "set up" by royal favors. His arrival and departure are usually on a much more humble scale.

I would tell you of the jackal lullabies, by which I am frequently soothed to sleep, and especially of the jackal concert one night at Ajmeer, where it seemed as if a thousand tom-cats were howling about the tent in which I slept. You see there is room for some picturesque happenings in the interstices between Christian Endeavor meetings.

XXI

CHRISTIAN ENDEAVOR IN HISTORIC INDIA

SATURDAY morning, January 9, found me in Agra; as usual, arriving at a new place long before daylight. But after a little time I found a warm welcome awaiting me in the home of Rev. J. G. Potter, of the English Baptist mission. Here, too, I saw for the first time Rev. A. G. McGaw, to whom Christian Endeavor in northern India is so much indebted.

Agra, you know, is the city of the Taj and of the Pearl Mosque and of the silver bathroom, and of ever so many other wonderful creations of that great architectural wizard, Shah Jehan. These have made Agra, in some respects, the most wonderful city in the world. So we stole a few hours for sight-seeing.

The Agra meetings, five in all, were profitable and helpful gatherings, the friends who came from the Presbyterian mission of Furruckabad contributing not a little to their value, as did also Miss Wrigler and other members of the Baptist Zenana Mission of Agra. Several of the missionaries came on their bicycles from their homes sixty miles away. The splendid roads of India, kept in perfect repair by the

MARBLE SCREEN IN PALACE IN DELHI

British government, are exactly fitted to the "silent steed." So, Christian Endeavorers, when you join the missionary forces of India, take your Columbias, or your Victors, or whatever may be "the very best wheel in the world,"—the one you ride, I mean.

Two of the Agra meetings were held in the Havelock Baptist Chapel, a place of sacred interest to me, for this church was founded more than sixty years ago, by the great Christian soldier and hero, Sir Henry Havelock, when he was stationed at Agra. Here he frequently preached, and here, most fittingly, in this chapel called by his name, his statue looks down week by week on the assembled Christian Endeavorers. I am sure, were he alive to-day, he would be an Endeavorer of heroic mould.

Delhi is scarcely second in historic interest to Agra, and every street of the old town is alive with memories of the terrible siege of the mutiny days. Here still stands the magnificent palace of the weak old Grand Mogul, who was led by his more strong-minded wives into a futile but terribly costly resistance to British arms. Here are the walls, still standing, pierced and battered by the shot and shell which tell of those awful days. But all is peaceful now, and, looking on the eager crowd of dark faces at the Christian Endeavor meetings in the Baptist mission church, you would have found it hard to believe that some of the most cruel deeds in all history were enacted scarcely a stone's throw away.

For these good meetings Christian Endeavorers must thank Rev. S. S. Thomas and Rev. Herbert Thomas and the ladies of the Zenana mission of Delhi.

One day in Delhi, one long night in the train, and in the shivery gray of a frosty morning twilight we find ourselves in Lahore, the capital of the great province of the Punjab. Your good friend and mine, Mr. McGaw, is with me now for the rest of the journey in north India. He is one of the most devoted, modest, and earnest of men. Now I can use the pronoun "we" without any poetic or editorial license.

Lahore is not only a great political centre, but a great missionary centre as well, especially for the American Presbyterians. Two days the Endeavorers stayed together here, and, by beginning very early in the mornings, managed to find room for eight Christian Endeavor meetings.

More like a genuine Christian Endeavor convention was this than any other meeting I have yet seen in India. Delegates had come from a dozen different societies, some even from the famous Mussoorie Union in the hills, a good thirty-six hours away by rail. The atmosphere was warm and cordial, and, from the opening devotional meeting to the solemn consecration service at the close, it was a meeting to be remembered.

Most delightful was the spirit of deep devotion displayed at every service. This mission has evidently had a peculiar spiritual blessing.

The convention was also particularly fortunate in the presence of Dr. John Henry Barrows, who not only in Lahore, but in Delhi, spoke glowing and eloquent words for Christian Endeavor. You will all be glad to know that Dr. Barrows's lectures in India are most favorably received, and are doing much good. The prejudice and misunderstanding which at first existed concerning his work have disappeared, and his eloquence and sweet Christian spirit have won their way to all hearts.

How I should like to introduce you all personally to the Ewings, and to Mr. Velte, and Mr. Hyde, and Dr. Orbison, and Mrs. and Miss Strahan of Mussoorie, and ever so many others! There were even two Juniors from Landour at the meeting. By the way, when you go to "San Francisco, '97," look for a tall, broad-shouldered, eloquent delegate from India, and you will see Rev. J. C. R. Ewing, D. D., of Lahore.

While we were at Lahore, the blessed rain came down from heaven upon the parched and hungry ground. Did you ever, in your dreams even, imagine a starving nation? India is that to-day. One hungry man excites our sympathy at home. Here are hungry millions of the famished. For twelve good hours during the convention it rained as it had not rained for months. "It is raining gold," said a native. It saved tens of thousands of lives undoubtedly in that one province, though it was not a general rain.

While the showers of blessing were descending within our Christian Endeavor convention hall, the other showers of blessings were descending outside; and for both we thanked God.

Some of our gospel hymns will mean more to me hereafter than ever before,—

> "Lord, I hear of showers of blessing
> Thou art scattering full and free,
> Showers the thirsty land refreshing;
> Let some droppings fall on me."

> "Send showers of blessing,
> Send showers refreshing,
> Send us showers of blessing,
> Send them, Lord, we pray."

XXII

A CHRISTIAN ENDEAVOR MEETING IN THE TAJ MAHAL

Christian Endeavor meetings have been held in all sorts of unlikely places.

I once attended one in the hollow trunk of a big tree in California. I have kneeled with other Endeavorers in the contracted cabin of a Japanese steamer. I have seen the "prayer shelf" which some earnest Juniors of Turkey mounted that they might find a place for their meeting, and also the bare, hot hillside, baked in the glare of centuries of Indian sunshine, where some Juniors of western India draw near to God.

But the most wonderful spot for an Endeavor meeting was the Taj Mahal, of Agra. Perhaps to say that here on the ninth of January, 1897, was held a meeting of Endeavorers, is more correct than to say that it was strictly an Endeavor meeting; but more of that later.

It is not too much to say that the Taj is the most exquisite building in all the world. Architects and artists, as well as common, every-day travellers like myself, admit this fact.

It stands on the banks of the sacred Jumna,

and was built by the famous Shah Jehan as a tomb for his beloved wife Mumtaz. It cost twenty millions of dollars. But these figures give no idea of its real value, or of the wealth lavished upon it, until we remember that even paid labor in India at the present time costs only seven or eight cents a day, and that the Taj was built largely by forced labor for which nothing was paid.

Twenty thousand men worked for twenty-two years to make this the grandest and most exquisite tomb that poor mortality ever occupied.

It is entirely of white marble, from the lowest course to the topmost pinnacle of the majestic dome, which seems to soar like a mighty bubble toward the sky. So kindly has the climate of India dealt with the Taj, that, though the year 1898 marks the quarter-millennial of its completion, you would think that only two hundred and fifty days instead of two hundred and fifty years had passed over its spotless dome, so unstained and unmarred is it by the hand of time.

You approach the Taj through a magnificent gateway of red sandstone and white marble, a building which, anywhere else in the world, would of itself be a marvel worth a thousand miles of travel to see. Just within this gateway you find yourself at the edge of a long and lovely garden filled with orchids and roses and brilliant flowers which we never see in a temperate clime. Palms and orange-trees and huge banyans compete with humbler shrubs to add their beauty to the garden. Down the centre runs a long, shallow marble basin, perhaps five hundred feet in length, filled with goldfish and silverfish, while green parrots and brilliant tropical birds of a hundred sorts flash through the checkered shade and sunlight of the garden.

This garden is kept in perfect condition by the British government, which fortunately now has possession of the Taj. At the end of this vista of perfect loveliness rises this exquisite dream in white marble, absolutely the most faultless and perfectly satisfying building in all the world.

> "Hushed, you advance, your gaze still fixed; heart, soul,
> Full of the wonder; drinking in its spell
> Of purity and mystery, its poise
> Magical, weird, aërial; the ghost
> Of thought draped white—as if that Sultan's sigh
> Had lived in issuing from his love and grief
> Immense, and taken huge embodiment,
> Which one rash word might change from tomb to cloud."

As we approach nearer, we see that what at first looked like fleckless marble is made still more beautiful by exquisite tracery of inlaid stones and gems. It is as if the jeweller's art had combined with the architect's skill to produce the eighth wonder of the world.

Some of the inlaid work represents passages from the Koran; elsewhere it is in the shape of scrolls and sprays of flowers most delicately colored, a hundred gems sometimes being used in making a single rose. All this marvellous tracery is scattered over the immense building in such lavish profusion and yet such exquisite taste that you almost hold your breath in wonder.

Out of the glare of the intolerable sun beating down pitilessly upon the white marble we pass within the ever open portal, through an inner screen of lacelike marble, and find ourselves at the tomb itself of the beautiful queen. This is in the exact centre of the building, while at one side, and raised a little higher, is the tomb of Shah Jehan himself. Both of these tombs are sprinkled thick with inlaid jewels.

> "Blown tulip and closed rose, lilies and vines,
> All done in cunning, finished jewelry
> Of precious gems—jasper and lazulite,
> Sardonyx, onyx, bloodstone, golden stone,
> Carnelian, jade, crystal and chalcedony,
> Turquoise and agate, and the berries and fruits
> Heightened with coral points and nacre lights;
> One single spray set here with fivescore stones;
> So that this place of death is made a bower
> With beauteous grace of blossoms overspread;
> And she who loved her garden lieth now
> Lapped in a garden. And all this for love!"

In this inner tomb was the little Christian Endeavor meeting held. There were twelve or thirteen of us,—Mr. and Mrs. Potter, of the English Baptist Mission of Agra; Mr. and Mrs. McGaw, Mr. and Mrs. Andrews, Mr. and Mrs. Bandy, Miss Bailey, Miss Forman, of the American Presbyterian Mission, who had come to Agra for the Christian Endeavor meetings; Mrs. McIntosh and Miss Wrigley, and other ladies of the Baptist Zenana Mission.

We were all seated upon the tombs. Overhead soared the vast dome, two hundred feet above our heads. So perfect is this dome that every sound uttered within the tomb is echoed and reëchoed, and echoed again, a hundred times, until it dies away in the vast bubble. Especially are high musical tones reproduced in a most weirdly marvellous way, until you almost think that a choir of ten thousand angels has taken up the song, and is chanting the refrain begun on earth.

No light and trivial tune or unworthy jig can here be given with good effect, but the sweet strains of some of our better popular hymns are reproduced with wonderful power. Mrs. Potter is gifted with a sweet soprano voice and under her leadership we sung,—

"Steal away, steal away, steal away to Jesus."

Slowly the strains of this pathetic old negro

melody seemed to "steal away" to the roof of the great dome. Then in softer cadence they were reflected back to us. They struck the side of the great marble balloon, and came back once more, and then again and yet again, but every time distinctly and clearly, until the air was full of "steal away," "steal away," "steal away," "steal away," "to Jesus," "to Jesus," "to Jesus," "to Jesus," loud and soft and remote and near. The effect was indescribable, and lovely beyond measure.

Then we sung "At the cross," and then all joined in repeating the Twenty-third Psalm. As some other visitors entered the Taj at that moment, and we did not wish to intrude upon them in a public place, we closed our little meeting.

Though it was a Mohammedan tomb, the surroundings were not so inappropriate as one might think, for on the tomb of Mumtaz herself are engraved the ninety-nine names which the Moslems have for God. Over the great gateway is written, in Persian characters, "The pure of heart shall enter the gardens of God"; and in this house of death itself is inscribed this beautiful sentiment from the Koran: "Saith Jesus (on whom be peace): 'This world is a bridge; pass thou over it, but build not upon it. This world is one hour; give its minutes to thy prayers; for the rest is unseen.'"

Christian Endeavor meetings have been held in many a beautiful temple before, but never, I think, in such a wondrous tomb temple as the Taj Mahal.

XXIII

CHRISTIAN ENDEAVOR ON THE GANGES

SATURDAY, January 17, found us at Fatehgarh, a city on the banks of the Ganges, and a sort of Mecca for me, on this Christian Endeavor pilgrimage. Here is a colony of four missionary families of the Presbyterian mission, the two Formans, a name fragrant in missionary annals in India, the McGaws, and the Bandys, two of the most prominent Christian Endeavorers of India. Mr. and Mrs. Andrews, too, ran down on their wheels, a little matter of forty miles, from another station.

When Sunday morning came, we all repaired, bright and early, to the mission church; and there indeed a Christian Endeavor welcome awaited us. Over the arched gateway was the word "Welcome," both in English and in Hindustanee. By the way, when next you come to see me at my house, you will find yourself welcomed in the same words, in the graceful, flowing Persian characters, as well as in thirteen other languages, over the front porch.

Within the church, too, was every outward and visible sign of the inward and spiritual greetings. The church looked like a beautiful garden, with its palms and bamboos and brilliant flowers of various hues, while behind the pulpit were banners and streamers with familiar mottoes, "HIND MASEH KA HOWE," "India for Christ," "MASIH AUR KALISYIA KELIYE," "For Christ and the church," in the Romanized Urdu character. I begged two of the mottoes for "San Francisco, '97," so that you as well as myself might have the benefit of them.

It has been my pleasant fortune to receive many greetings on your behalf, my fellow Endeavorers, in many languages; but I do not remember when I have ever before received from a bard a welcome in Persian verse. To be sure, I could not understand it; and I had to beg from the poet a translation of his verses. At the same place, also, I received the gavel and block, studded with native state rupees of silver, which are to be used in calling to order the convention at San Francisco next July. These were presented by the wide-awake and ever-enterprising local union of Mussoorie, the hill station where the missionaries congregate in the summer.

We had two pleasant meetings in this church, and no one could ever have had so good an interpreter, it seems to me, as it was my good fortune to have in Rev. John Forman, a missionary's son, who was born and bred in the country, and has now come back to take his father's place. Almost before the words came from my lips he would take them up and translate them into beautiful and fluent Hindustanee without hesitation or break, so that it seemed almost like one continuous speech in two different languages. O that some of the interpreters from whom I have suffered many things in many lands could have heard this brilliant feat in translation, so that they might realize what it is to enter into the spirit as well as into the mere verbal performance of an interpreter's task!

But the pleasantest day must come to an end, and so did this delightful Sunday. The next day found us pushing on to Allahabad, a great central city of India. Here are two Christian Endeavor societies, one in the Methodist and one in the Baptist church; and two very pleasant meetings we had, in both of which I could use my mother tongue, and speak in the best English, or, rather, the best Americanese, I could muster.

The society in the Methodist church is one of the oldest in India, and to the hospitable parsonage of Mr. Clancy I was welcomed again, as on a previous visit. Mr. and Mrs. Clancy were away at the annual conference of their church, but they had left some good representatives in their stead, and the reception which followed the evening address was one of the most pleasant of social occasions.

Benares is only three hours by rail from Allahabad, and here we were welcomed by the representatives of the London Missionary Society, though as yet there are no Christian Endeavor societies in the sacred city. During the twenty-four hours in Benares two good meetings in the interest of Christian Endeavor were held. One was for the Hindustanee Christians, at which I was assisted by another most admirable interpreter, Mr. Mookerjee, the head master of the high school. A drawing-room reception and meeting for all the missionaries of the station, was also held in the hospitable and spacious parlors of the bungalow of the London Missionary Society. A thousand thanks to my kind friends who have made these memorable days so profitable to the cause of Christian Endeavor,—a vote of thanks in which a million Christian Endeavorers, I am sure, will join. Is the motion carried? I think I hear you all say, "Ay."

XXIV

AN HOUR ON THE GANGES

In some quarters the idea seems to prevail that one religion is quite as good as another; that Christianity is merely a cult derived from the fathers, and largely a matter of heredity and environment, but that Hinduism is quite as good for India, and Buddhism for China, as Christianity for America.

I should like to take Christians of this flabby, jelly-fish structure on a personally conducted visit to Benares, the most sacred city of all the world to the Hindus. To this city more millions of human hearts turn as to their Mecca than to any other city in the world. Here we find Hinduism in its most orthodox form—in all its loathsomeness and corruption. It is the metropolis of the Hindu faith. In all its filth and utter vileness can heathenism here be studied as nowhere else in the world. It is the most characteristic of heathen cities. Hinduism is not distorted or exaggerated, it simply comes to its rank and poisonous flower and fruitage.

Let us take one of the many boats that are tied to the shores of the Ganges, and float slowly down the sacred stream before the palaces and temples. First we come to a great bathing-ghat, as it is called, where hundreds of men and women are engaged in washing away the vilest character stains in the holy river. The water is foul and muddy enough, in all conscience, and would seem to leave more spots than it would cleanse; but into it wade boldly the devout pilgrims, laving in and lapping eagerly the filthy stream. Behind the walls of the palaces which line the banks of the stream, we are told, are " multitudes of aged people, come together from all parts of India, waiting with calm, patient, ecstatic happiness the summons of the Angel of Death; for he who is fortunate enough to die in Benares goes straight to glory."

As we glide down the river we see many fakirs, with long, matted, rope-like locks, their bodies smeared with white ashes, looking like bleached corpses rather than healthy human beings. There is one fakir standing on one leg. How long he stands! Two, three, five, ten minutes! Our bones ache in sympathy with his, but he is winning priceless years of glory by this act of devotion.

There is another fakir doubling himself up in a most absurd and ludicrous way,—if one has the heart to see the ludicrous side of things amid such surroundings. First he touches the top of his crown to the soil. Then he lays himself out at full length on the dusty bank. Then he doubles himself up, as you would believe only a practised acrobat could do, until his head appears between his distended legs, and his shoulder-blades scrape the dusty soil. He is one of the preachers of this Eastern faith; and the thought irresistibly occurs to one, What a tremendous audience could our sensational ministers at home draw, if they would but take lessons of this acrobatic Hindu preacher!

And there is a boy of twelve or fifteen washing his sins away in the same holy stream. From the top of his head, which otherwise is shaven close, hangs a long lock of black hair, —the lock by which he believes the good angel will seize him, when he is hanging over the brink of perdition, and drag him back into Paradise.

Some of the pilgrims are not only using the holy water for cleansing purposes, but a kind of fuller's earth as well, in lieu of soap. They will not use soap because it contains animal fat.

As we leave the river, and mount the steep and dirty steps, we come very soon to the very holy of holies of Benares, the famous temple of the awful Siva. This is called the Golden Temple, though there is very little gold about it, two of the turrets only being gilded with the precious metal.

Here is the very centre and essence of Hinduism. A marble slab upon the wall tells us that those who do not profess the Hindu religion are requested not to enter the temple; but we are allowed to go upon a neighboring house-top and look down within its dirty precincts. The marble floor of the temple is absolutely thick with mud and offal, the bare feet of the worshippers leaving a momentary white track upon the pavement, which the thick ooze soon covers.

More than any other god, Siva, we are told, "is cruel, and exacts a bloody worship. He is the ruler of evil spirits, ghouls, and vampires, and at nightfall he prowls about in their company in places of execution and where there are buried dead. He is the god, too, of mad, frantic folly, who, clothed in the bloody skin of an elephant, leads the wild dance of Tandava. He is the god of the Ascetics. This fearful sect go naked, smutty with ashes, their long matted hair twisted around their heads. Others follow hideous secret rites of blood, lust, gluttony, drunkenness, and incantations. Others pose themselves in immovable attitudes till the sinews shrink and the posture becomes rigid. Others tear their bodies with knives, or devour carrion or excrements."

Such is the chief god of the Golden Temple of Benares, and such is the object of devoutest

Hindu worship. But the Golden Temple is not the only one in Benares, by any means. There are hundreds of other little temples wedged into every conceivable nook of the holy city. Great temples claiming their worshippers by thousands; monkey temples, about which the simian caricatures of humanity scamper and grin at the spectators, for all the world as though they were on exhibition in Central Park or the Philadelphia Zoo.

Another temple which every traveller visits is that of the Goddess of Plenty, the patroness of beggars. Around the doors of this temple are scores of mendicants with their bowls, waiting for the handfuls of rice which the devout worshipper is sure to throw them, while, within, the temple is filled with sacred bulls and cows, whose ordure and uncleansed filth make it extremely uninviting to sight and smell. In fact, so utterly filthy is the floor of this temple that one does not venture within, though he is freely allowed to enter, but contents himself with a glimpse from a side door. No self-respecting American farmer would allow his barnyard or his cow-house floor to become as filthy as this most sacred temple.

But we cannot go the rounds of all these sacred spots this morning; it would take days and weeks to "do" them thoroughly; what we have seen shows us the genius of Hinduism, much vaunted, widely lauded Hinduism,—the religion which some æsthetic Americans, ever itching for a new sensation, have thought might take the place of the religion of Christ, or at least take its place side by side with the faith of the lowly Nazarene.

Contrast for a single moment the religion of the Bible with the religion of Benares,—the temple of the Holy Ghost with the temple of Siva, the stone bull, dirty with the dust and grease of ages, with the Christian's conception of the Lamb of God who taketh away the sins of the world. In fact, the only antidote needed to the claims of the lackadaisical toleration of all religions as equally uplifting to the race, is an hour on the Ganges or among the temples of Benares.

XXV

THE FAMINE AT SHORT RANGE

In the lands of the Occident hunger is almost an unknown thing. To be sure, we have the perpetually hungry small boy. He is ever with us. But his hunger is of the healthy and wholesome sort, and a plate of cakes is a panacea for all his troubles.

One often sees, too, the professional beggar with the stereotyped plea of hunger and starvation, with the seven small children waiting at home for the daily crust. When the seven small children are investigated, however, it is often found that they are mythical characters, and that the starvation plea is assumed as part of his stock in trade.

Of course I am not saying that there is not real destitution and actual hunger found occasionally among the very poor in the great cities of both America and Great Britain. But these cases are so sporadic and exceptional that they give us no idea of the dreadfulness of famine.

But in India to-day the famine is not a mere sentiment, not a far-away abstraction, not even a dreadful possibility, but an actual and terrible reality.

A single hungry man or woman is a pitiable object. If such a one is found in the country districts of old England or New England, how the provisions flow in upon him! Apples and potatoes, flour and bacon, and any quantity of the good things of life, make his heart glad; and a thrill of horror would be felt by every one in the community if it were thought that there was a starving man at their doors.

But multiply one starving man by a thousand, and then multiply this thousand by a thousand more, and this million by ten again, and then you have scarcely compassed the number of the hungry men, women, and children in the great empire of India. Not that so great a number is starving, but all are suffering more or less from privation.

But these figures can give a very faint idea of the real horrors of the situation. One must actually see the gaunt and hungry faces, the bony arms and legs from which every particle of tissue has wasted away; one must look into the hollow eyes, and see the skeleton-like breasts on which every rib stands out like the ribs of an umbrella; one must see the pitiable hands stretched out for a handful of grain, and see the wretched recipients gulp it down with famished eagerness, unground and uncooked. Then, after seeing one such throng as this, let him try to realize that he has but seen one or two hundreds of the millions who are suffering from the pangs of hunger, and, ever after, famine becomes a real and dreadful thing to him.

In many parts of India I have seen the relief works started by the government; for, had it not been for the foresight and enterprise of the British government, the suffering would have been far worse than it is. Everywhere relief works have been opened, and, as you drive along the dusty highways, you see hundreds, and sometimes thousands, of people in the fields gathering stones, and other hundreds breaking them into small pieces for the excellent macadamized roads which are found throughout India. In fact, the government has on hand in many parts of the country a stock of road material which it cannot use for years. But the object is not so much to build roads, or to keep them in repair, as to provide work and wages for the hungry road makers.

Of course when there are so many needy ones the money must be made to go as far as possible, and no extravagant wages are paid these road-builders. The able-bodied men receive two annas (two pence) for a day's work; the women, one anna (one penny); the children, six pies (a half-penny); and even the babies in arms, who are brought to the field of operation, though their puny little arms could not lift a pebble as big as a walnut, are entered upon the list of famine-relief laborers, and are gravely paid at the end of the twenty-four hours one pice (one farthing) for their day's labor.

Many hundreds of thousands, if not millions, are now enrolled by the government in these relief works, and the number is constantly increasing. No applicant, worthy or unworthy, is turned away. If only he has the passport of genuine want and hunger, he is given something to do, and receives his penny at the day's end. Even in this land of cheap prices it must not be supposed that for two annas one can fare sumptuously every day; but that sum will buy enough of the cheaper sort of grain to keep the wolf from the door, or, rather, partially to satisfy the intolerable craving of hunger.

All our Western similes and figures of speech seem absolutely inadequate to the occasion. For instance, the one I have just used, of the wolf at the door, is absurdly tame. The wolf of hunger is always at the door of most of the hovels of India. The poor people never think of driving him far away. They simply "shoo" him from the door-step, as the old housewife would scare away the too familiar chickens that intrude upon her domain; but as for actually keeping the wolf out of sight, it is an unheard-of thing in India. Every year there is more or less famine in some section of the country. Every year the crops fail somewhere, and, though the wise forethought of a paternal government, and the multiplication of railways, and hence the ability to transport grain swiftly from one part of the country to another, have greatly diminished the danger and the suffering, yet in the best of years many parts of India are always on famine's ragged edge.

The most pathetic sight which I have witnessed in India was a crowd of hungry beggars that gathered one Sunday afternoon near the mission bungalow of Rev. Mr. Wharton, in Harda in the Central Provinces. Along the roadside were these dreadful skeletons, lining the pathway to the house for fully an eighth of a mile, crowded together on each side as thickly as they could "squat." Destitution and suffering were written on every face. Some doubtless were professional beggars; but even professional beggars may be hungry, and the eager way in which they snatched the handful of grain which we were able to give them showed that starvation was to them a very real and dreadful thing.

Almost more pitiable than the human suffering is that of the poor starved beasts that cannot speak for themselves. All over India the "gharrie" horses have felt the famine most bitterly; the prices of grain and fodder have everywhere risen enormously; the masters are fain to eat the husks, or rather the poor and cheap grain which otherwise they would give to the beasts of labor, and often the poor horse goes hungry.

Such bags of bones, such travesties of horses, such slow-moving horse-like quadrupeds, I never saw outside of this dry and thirsty land. The blows of the drivers resounding from their hollow ribs send a throb of pity to every compassionate heart, and one longs for a Mr. Bergh or a Mr. Angell to arise for India, and to inaugurate "the society with the long name" in every village and hamlet.

The only thing that the Hindus can think of doing to avert the famine is to pray to their rain-god for relief. Wherever the rain-god has a temple, he is this year drenched in water to remind him of the dry weather outside his temple.

Sometimes, indeed, he is immersed in a tank of water, so that he may become thoroughly wet through, and thus be inclined to relieve the drought. But alas! alas! in many parts of India the heavens are still as brass, and no showers of blessing fall on the parched ground.

In some places, however, the winter rains have come, and O how refreshing they are! No one outside of arid India can realize what they mean. "It is raining gold," said a Hindu, as the showers began to fall in the Punjab; "it is raining gold "; and so, indeed, it was. But, though the rains may come and relieve to some extent the suffering, there will still be a vast amount of misery this year and next as well. Everywhere Christian hearts should be open, and Christian pockets as well, to give generously to this famine-stricken people, and may the bread of wheat and corn which the people receive open their hearts to receive the Bread of life, the true bread which came down from heaven, which if a man eat he shall never die.

XXVI

ROCKED ON THE BOSOM OF THE GANGES

How shall I describe these recent days, my dear fellow travellers? As I write, I am being rocked on the broad bosom of the Ganges in a missionary house-boat on which we are slowly making the journey, towed by coolies, up into the heart of the delta of the Ganges, where the Bengalee Christian Endeavor convention for which we are bound is to be held.

I could fill a small volume with the novel and unique experiences of the last two days; but then, to make them vivid, I should need not only to use my Bull's-eye camera, and to get the publishers to allow me to fill my book full of snap-shots from cover to cover, but I should also need the brush of an artist to paint the cocoanut-palms, the date-trees and bananas along the banks; the gorgeous birds that flit through the trees, and the still more gorgeous natives, in mahogany skins and red, orange, green, and white cloths, that line the banks, and fill the narrow streets of the straw-built villages that we are continually passing.

I am quite in despair about taking you with me in any adequate, satisfactory way on this, the most novel Christian Endeavor journey I have ever taken. However, here are the bare facts. We left Calcutta in the evening by train, and after riding all night we reached Khoolna on the Ganges, where there awaited us a little stern-wheel steamer, which kicked the water out behind with a vigorous splash.

Just at dawn it started. The owls were hooting their last hoot for the night; the jackals were slinking away from the daylight, and all the rest of the world was waking up to begin a new day.

This whole country is a perfect lace-work of waterways, great and small. The Ganges discharges its immense volume of water, borne down from the snowy Himalayas, through a dozen different mouths, each of them a wide estuary of onrushing water. Between these large streams are innumerable little creeks and canals, through which our steamer threads its way, sometimes under the overhanging branches of palms and plantains, which sweep the deck with their laden boughs. The streams, little or big, are alive with boats large and small, and the boats are alive with men and women and boys and girls.

Our little steamer makes great havoc among them in the narrow canals, first sucking away the water from beneath their keels, and then tossing them up, sometimes high and dry on

A HIGH-CASTE CARRIAGE IN CENTRAL INDIA

A SACRED FAKIR. HE HAS TAKEN A VOW TO LIVE IN THIS SWING

A PET GAZELLE IN THE ANIMAL HOSPITAL

A HALF-DESERTED STREET IN BOMBAY DURING THE PLAGUE

SOME OF DR CLARK'S SNAPSHOTS

the low shore, as the water rushes back. When they see us coming, the boatmen all scramble on board pell-mell, and hold on to their frail craft for dear life, until the steam monster, which so disturbs their placid waters, has rushed by.

Thus all day long we journey until evening shades infold us and the steamer draws near to Barisal. Look! what is that line of wavering light coming down the village street between the mud huts? Nothing more nor less, my fellow travellers, than a torchlight procession of Christian Endeavorers coming down to the wharf to meet us; for Christian Endeavor has found its way into the swamps of the Ganges, and is a living, vital force here.

Soon we were in the comfortable bungalow of Rev. William Carey, a great-grandson of the great missionary of the same name, who is working out the Christian Endeavor problem for India more fully than any one else. He has already formed more than sixty Endeavor societies in this one field, and all within two years. Who in all the world has a record better than that?

Let me introduce him to you,—this William Carey, the second, who will always be dear to Christian Endeavorers, as his great-grandfather is to all the Christian world. He is not a tall man or a giant in stature; but, as you can imagine, a man *alive* every inch of him, from crown to toe. With black hair and eyes and black mustache he seems the very personification of energy and vitality. When he speaks in public, he talks all over, and not with slow and languid speech. Even his coat-tails grow eloquent, as used to be said of John B. Gough. This is the man whom God has used so greatly, and whose whole soul is enlisted in the cause of Christian Endeavor.

"Carey Sahib very good man; Mem Sahib very good woman," said the little Mohammedan skipper of our steamer, as we drew near the mission bungalow, and we were prepared to echo this description before we had been five minutes under their hospitable roof. The next morning early, before starting up the Ganges on our long twenty-four hours' journey into the swamps, we attended a united meeting of the girls' and young women's societies of Barisal. A more interesting congregation you could not wish to see; a good example this of the material Christian Endeavor has to work upon in Bengal, and of the work it is able to do.

The members of the older society have four pices a month for spending-money. Now four pices amount to the munificent sum of two cents, which must last them thirty days; but out of this these generous Endeavorers support a colporteur, who distributes about eight thousand tracts a month to the passengers on the many river steamers that touch at Barisal. Many of the girls give not a tenth, but *all* their spending-money every month. The little girls have a missionary garden where they raise vegetables; and some months, by laboring hard, they have managed to make four annas (eight cents) as the contribution of their society. These are not the widow's mites, but the maidens' mites. Hear the Lord of the treasury: " Verily I say unto you that these poor maidens have cast more in than all they which have cast into the treasury. For all they did cast in of their abundance, but they of their want did cast in all that they had."

Now we are off, as I told you at the beginning, for a twenty-four-hour convention away among "the Bheels." But, as Rudyard Kipling says, " that is another story."

XXVII

A MISSIONARY MECCA

One of our many pilgrimages in India which I did not have time to tell you about in chronological order and in detail, because Christian Endeavor events pressed upon me at the time so thick and fast, was a visit to Serampore, twelve miles from Calcutta, the scene of the life-work of the pioneer missionaries, Carey, Marshman, and Ward.

Many of you will remember that the British East India Company would not allow Carey to work in Calcutta, or on any part of the soil of India controlled by them; but Serampore then belonged to Denmark, and the Danish governor welcomed him.

Here in the college founded by Carey is a flourishing Christian Endeavor society, of which I have before written, and every rood of that historic ground is fragrant with memories of the great Endeavorer.

We were kindly met at the station by one of the younger missionaries, who proved to be a most excellent guide.

First we were taken to the cemetery,—sacred soil, indeed; for here, with many other missionary compatriots, lie William Carey, Marshman, Ward, and a child of Adoniram Judson's.

Carey's tomb is a somewhat imposing monument of brick and plaster, still in very good preservation. It was erected by himself on the death of his first wife, and on one side, after his own death, this inscription was carved at his own request:—

WILLIAM CAREY,

BORN 17 AUGUST, 1761.   DIED 9 JUNE, 1834.

A WRETCHED, POOR, AND HELPLESS WORM,

ON THY KIND ARMS I FALL.

The tombs of Marshman and Ward, who, during their lifetime, were scarcely less useful than Carey himself, are of very similar construction, and occupy even more conspicuous positions in the cemetery, Carey's being in one corner near the entrance.

The great college building, with its imposing colonnade, its massive pillars, and its superb view of the Ganges River, over whose banks it stands, is, however, Carey's greatest monument. Here are his literary remains, though his mortal remains moulder in the graveyard near by. In the great college library are the many versions of the Scriptures which this indefatigable scholar produced. Shelf after shelf is filled with them; no less than forty different languages and dialects are represented, as his great-grandson told me.

Many of these Carey had printed at his own expense, and the college building itself was erected largely by his own means, for as professor of Sanskrit in the college of Fort Edward he received five thousand rupees (more than two thousand dollars) a month. Out of this he spent about one hundred rupees for himself, and gave away the rest. There was a tithe-giver for you, indeed! One-fiftieth of his income he spent on himself; the other forty-nine fiftieths he gave to the Lord's work.

But, after all, I think the building that most interested me in Serampore was not the imposing college or the well-kept tomb, but an old, dilapidated Hindu temple on the banks of the Ganges.

For a hundred years, I suppose, this temple has not been used for heathen worship. At least, it was deserted and ruined in Carey's time, as it is to-day. At one time during Carey's residence, Henry Martyn, that other heaven-sent missionary, spent some months in Serampore. Desiring a place for secret prayer where he could be quite undisturbed, he sought out this ruined pagoda, and there would spend the early morning hour. Carey, Marshman, and Ward heard of this strange prayer-room of their friend, and sometimes they would join

Martyn at his devotions; and, when Judson visited Serampore, he, too, naturally joined the group.

Think of that scene in the old ruined temple, now fast falling to complete decay, a great pepul-tree forcing its giant roots and branches through the very walls; the Ganges River rolling hard by;—Martyn, Judson, Carey (the great trio of modern missions), Marshman, Ward (making up a noble quintette), raising their united voices to Almighty God for a redeemed India! The imagination is stirred and the pulses thrilled by this mental picture, even after the lapse of eighty years.

But there is another object which should not be omitted from a truthful picture of Serampore. In a public square, not a pistol-shot from Carey's grave, stands a huge car of Juggernaut, sixty feet high, built in many stories, and covered with strange, rude paintings. In a temple near by sits Juggernaut himself, with round, staring eyes as big as saucers, a half-moon mouth painted red, and a hideous nose, a scarlet petticoat of red calico covering him from neck to feet. Altogether, he is one of the most grotesque and ugly gods I have seen in all India; and that is saying a great deal.

Once a year he is given a bath with Ganges water, but the operation is so rare that he is supposed to catch cold and fall sick; so he is taken out of his temple for an airing. A great rope is hitched to his neck, and a dozen men haul him up to the top of his car, which stands near by. Then a thousand men grasp the ropes tied to the car, and tug and strain to pull the gigantic carriage of the god along the heavy, sandy road.

The moral of these contrasted scenes? There are enough of them. Here is one: Carey's work, so well begun, is not yet fully done. The master workman dies, but the work, still unfinished, calls for other skilled and consecrated laborers. Juggernaut still sits in his temple. "No slacker grows the fight." Who will volunteer?

XXVIII

CONCERNING A UNIQUE AND MEMORABLE CONVENTION

I AM now on my way back from the most novel and one of the most interesting Christian Endeavor conventions I ever attended in my life.

The journey to the convention alone is worth chronicling at length. For three hours we journeyed on a Ganges River steamer. Then she tied up to a bank of slippery, salvy mud, where we were transferred to the missionary house-boat, and after a time were taken in tow by another steamer for three hours more.

Then our itinerating novelties began. The house-boat could go but a few yards up this stream, so we bundled ourselves and our belongings into a "dingey," a little boat about the size of a Charles River canoe, and quite as unsteady.

The dingey is decked over, and is covered with a hood of matting, under which one crawls on his hands and knees. There is no "standing-up" or "sitting-up room," but only "lying-down room," in a dingey. However, it was long after dark by the time we reached this stage of the journey; so it was quite time to lie down.

Thus we proceeded for about three hours more, when we reached an obstruction in the stream, which the dingey could not go around or over or under.

But my kind host, Mr. Carey, had provided for that; and on the bank were a dozen Endeavorers with two "palkees" or palanquins. Into the palanquin, which was only a piece of netting slung on a long bamboo pole, I squeezed myself, while the Endeavorers hoisted me upon their shoulders.

I felt like a trussed turkey with my knees doubled up to my chin. It was a well-meant kindness, but after a short ride of this sort, to show that I appreciated their trouble, I begged to be allowed to walk. This walk I greatly enjoyed, though the road was anything but a boulevard, and the dim light of the twinkling stars made the many bridges of a single plank over the intersecting stream somewhat fearsome.

However, the five miles were safely traversed, and then we crawled into another dingey for another three hours' ride. At last, at two o'clock in the morning, the convention village, Chhabikhàrpàr, was reached. This village is in the heart of the Bheels, and in the centre of a large Christian Bengalee community.

Already the Endeavorers had begun to gather, and in the chapel near by I could hear the sound of the cymbals and the tom-toms and the singing, as I dropped off for a few hours of sleep in the grass hut of one of the natives.

Morning came all too soon for tired humanity, and with its first dawn the opening of the convention; for the people must get home the same night, and a three days' convention was to be crowded into one, with an almost continuous session of twelve hours from dawn to dusk.

Let me picture our surroundings. Imagine a village of forty huts of mud and thatch, each about twelve or fifteen feet square and ten feet high, built around a muddy pond, or "tank," as it is called. The only door is a hole about two feet and a half square, and one is obliged to double up like a jackknife to get in. Until you almost stumble against one of the houses, you would scarcely know that there was a village near, for it is embowered in a forest of cocoanut-trees and plantains (banana-trees) and date-palms. About half the people of Chhabikhàrpàr are Christian and half heathen Hindus.

At one end of the village stands the chapel, which the people built with their own money, the best building in the village, with a good thatch roof and walls of wood reaching nearly to the roof. The road to the chapel is gay with plantain stalks and red Christian Endeavor banners, for all the fifty-five societies represented have brought at least one banner, and some four or five,—not very expensive flags, to be sure, usually only a yard of red calico with a Scripture verse in Bengalee characters upon it; but they all add to the picturesqueness of the scene.

And look! look! Of all the extraordinary scenes ever witnessed at a Christian Endeavor convention, that is the most extraordinary. With brass cymbals clanging, and native drums beating, and hands clapping, a society from a neighboring village comes dancing up to the chapel, with half a dozen red banners streaming before it. The leader, one of the territorial Christian Endeavor organizers, goes before to lead the procession, dancing backward, which is a very perilous operation on the narrow, uneven road, beating time, and singing a Christian hymn at the top of his lungs.

> "Jesus, O Jesus, come into my heart;
> The sight of thy beautiful face drives trouble away.
> O Jesus, come into my heart.
>
> "Jesus, O Jesus, come into my heart;
> When thou comest in, it is heaven on earth.
> O Jesus, come into my heart.

"Jesus, O Jesus, come into my heart;
Seeing thee, it is cool; seeing thee, it is cool.
O Jesus, come into my heart."

We should say, "Jesus *warms* my heart." In this hot clime he *cools* it. But, if their hearts were cool, their faces did not show it; for the perspiration dripped from the dancers as they reached the chapel.

Within the chapel the dance waxed warmer and more vigorous. Two Endeavorers, facing each other and flinging their arms in the air, would spring from side to side with marvellous agility, but never losing their self-poise or "the power" in all the excitement. Now the tune changes, and they sing,—

"The stream of love is flowing by;
The stream of love is flowing by,"

and by a wavy motion of the line they indicate the "stream of love."

Again a change, and they cry out,—

"There are *heaps* of love at the foot of the cross;
There are HEAPS of love at the foot of the cross,"

and with arms outstretched and arched over they show how it is "heaped up."

At last the song is over, and the dancers sink down upon their mats, squatting upon their heels, where they will remain immovable for the next three hours.

The leader then goes out, and dances another society into the chapel in the same vigorous way, and then another, and another, until the chapel is full.

Does any one object to this vigorous terpsichorean type of religion? I can only say that as actually witnessed I saw nothing objectionable in it, though perhaps my clumsy description may seem gross and uncouth. There was no "promiscuous mingling of the sexes," for all who danced were men. It seemed a real devotional act; and I understood, as never before, how David "danced before the Lord."

It is sufficient to say, perhaps, that the conservative Baptist mission of Bengal, the mission founded by William Carey, sees nothing to disapprove in this service.

After all were seated and the little chapel was crowded full of squatting figures, packed like sardines in a box, the banners of each society were presented, with a short address from the president of each. Some of the inscriptions on the banners were very significant, though I cannot give them here; but all told of faith and love and hope. Then followed addresses on different features of the pledge; for the Christian Endeavor pledge is found as indispensable in Bengal as in America. Songs were often interspersed, and there was a prayer chain in true Christian Endeavor fashion, and many little seasons of quiet devotion were enjoyed. Thus passed five or six hours of almost continuous service, when the hungry delegates took a recess of an hour in order to get something to eat. But they soon re-assembled for another session that lasted till dark.

There was not a little object-teaching by the missionaries.

For one exercise, Scripture verses bearing upon "love" were called for. They came thick and fast from the audience,—"God is love," "God so loved the world," etc. As fast as uttered they were written in Bengalee characters upon slips of colored paper, red and blue and green. These slips were then deftly made into a "chain of love," with the help of a little paste. Then a swarthy brother, a deacon in the Chhabikhàrpàr Church, of deep mahogany color, who was arrayed in his "birthday suit," and not a shred beside, with the exception of a scrap of cloth about his loins, came to the front, and with all the dignity of a full-dress ceremonial he put the garland of love about my neck. Had I been able to return the compliment with a Christian Endeavor pin, I could not have fastened it to him anywhere without hurting him.

Hundreds had come to the meeting who could not get into the chapel, or indeed anywhere near an open window, so the closing service was held in a wide rice-field near by. The closing consecration meeting was tender and solemn, and a time of great spiritual refreshment.

It was found that of the sixty-two societies in the district, fifty-five were represented by one hundred and twenty-six men and twenty-four women, besides the home societies and the crowds of other visitors. Some delegates walked for one or two days to get to the meeting. The missionaries present, Mr. Kerry, Mr. Teichmann, and Mr. Tragellus, were most helpful, as well as Mr. McGaw who accompanied me; and Rev. Mr. Carey's guiding hand was felt throughout the whole day. Yet it was a genuine Endeavor convention, and, better still, a Bengalee Endeavorers' convention, proving conclusively that Christian Endeavor can be adapted to "the Bheels" of Bengal as well as to the rectangular streets of Philadelphia. It was a convention never to be forgotten.

XXIX

THE SONG OF THE MURDERER OF THIRTY

IMAGINE the strangest Christian Endeavor convention you ever dreamed of, and you will not exaggerate in grotesqueness and strange interest the scene I am about to describe. It occurred in Chhabikhàrpàr in connection with the second Christian Endeavor convention of the East Bengal Union.

Scene: a rude chapel, with earthen floor and thatched roof,—the best building, however, in all the village,—a building erected by the native converts themselves, showing that they believe in giving the Lord of their very best.

Imagine this chapel packed with dark-skinned native Christians sitting immovably upon their heels and packed together almost as tightly as peas in a pod. Some of the delegates have little brass cymbals, which they clang together during the singing. Three or four drums about the size and shape of little nail-kegs contribute to the musical (?) effect. The different ends of the drum are tuned to different keys, so that in a sense the two ends accompany each other. No drumsticks are used, but the musicians play with their fingers and the balls of their hands.

Other musical instruments are used which are quite beyond my powers of description. They are played with a single string and a toothpick, and any one who likes this kind of music is welcome to the task of eulogizing it.

If the instrumental music is not altogether melodious to Western ears, the singing of the convention was exceedingly delightful. Few English tunes were sung; nor, indeed, need the Bengalee Christians be dependent on "Watts and Select" or Lowell Mason or Moody and Sankey, for their flowing musical Bengalee music is quite sufficient for all their needs.

A little pause came in the flag-presentation and prayers and addresses of the eleven hours' convention; and then the sweetest singer in all the company arose, and, joined by three or four others, whose voices harmonized with his own, waving his hands and keeping time with his feet, he sung "The Song of the Murderer of Thirty," a song of his own composing. It might better be called perhaps "The Name of Jesus," for the name that is above every name was the constantly recurring theme. This was the way it began:

> "O, the name of Jesus,
> It feels so good."

This is a literal translation of an otherwise inexpressible Bengalee phrase, but it is not very far removed from the psalmist's expression, "O *taste* and see that the Lord is good." Then the song goes on:—

"Who first sung the name?
 The angels in Bethlehem sang the name;
 Through this name heaven and earth come together.
 Through this name black and white meet together.
 Through this name Shadrach passed through the fire.
 Through this name Sankey and Moody aroused the people.
 Through this name George Müller conquered.
 Through this name the Murderer of Thirty received salvation."

Thus the song goes on. Each line is a distinct stanza, and requires with the chorus some time to sing.

There are now only thirty-two verses in the hymn; but there is no reason why one of these days there should not be one hundred and thirty-two, for accretions can be readily made, and all the list of worthies from Adam the First can be celebrated.

It may be noticed that Sankey's name comes first in this song, and not the usual order, "Moody and Sankey." I suppose the singer felt a special kinship for his fellow singer across the sea, and so honored him with the pre-eminence.

But who is the Murderer of Thirty?

Ah! this is a story well worth telling in plain prose, since I cannot aspire to poetic flights.

Here is the plain and unvarnished story as told me by the Bengalee author of the hymn and translated by a missionary. I wish I could picture the scene: the earnest, dark-skinned Christian telling the story with much gesture and dramatic effect, while I jotted down the translation in my note-book. On the Malabar coast lived a robber, fierce and implacable, who became in time a leader of a band of robbers. This band was the terror of the whole neighborhood, and in the course of their pillaging expeditions their leader, Kothabye by name, killed with his own hand thirty unoffending victims. After years of robbery and murder Kothabye was captured and sold as a slave. No one would keep him long, however, on account of his ugly and violent temper. So he changed from master to master, and on one occasion was found in the market-place loaded with chains and waiting for a purchaser.

In this pitiable plight a missionary saw him, and offered to purchase him if he could be had for a low price. At length, after some haggling, he was knocked down to the missionary for twelve rupees, about four dollars. The missionary took him to his bungalow, and there told him that he did not want him for a slave, but wished him to become Christ's freeman. As the missionary preached of forgiveness by

The Song of the Murderer

the blood of Christ, Kothabye interrupted him by saying, "But will he forgive a murderer?"

"Yes," said the missionary, "if the murderer is penitent."

"But will he forgive a man who has killed five men?" said Kothabye.

"Yes," answered the missionary.

"But will he forgive one who has killed ten?"

"Yes."

"But supposing one has committed twenty murders, can he be forgiven?"

"Yes," answered the missionary again.

"But if he has killed thirty men?"

"The blood of Jesus Christ will wash away all sins," said the missionary.

"Then he will save me," answered Kothabye, "for I am the Murderer of Thirty."

Then Kothabye began to pray; but he made so dreadful a noise, screaming and crying out for mercy in so frightful a way, that the missionary could not stand it. So Kothabye went off into the jungle where he could pray as loud as he pleased without disturbing any one. Here he found peace, and became a preacher of righteousness, and before he died between two and three thousand of the members of his tribe ascribed to him their conversion.

Well indeed might the sweet singer chant, "Through this name the Murderer of Thirty received salvation."

After this song and this story we could join even more heartily in the sentiment of the song that followed,—

> "There are heaps of love at the foot of the cross,
> There are heaps of love at the foot of the cross."

XXX

A LONG FORWARD STEP

My last week in northern India was a very busy one, and a very important one for Christian Endeavor in India; for during that week the " United Society of Christian Endeavor for India, Burmah, and Ceylon " was formed,—an organization which, I believe, will have as far-reaching and blessed consequences for India as the formation of the American United Society in 1885, or of the British Council of Christian Endeavor in 1392, if I have the year right.

Engagements in Calcutta were numerous and delightful, including a most pleasant reception in the Free Church Mission hall, where more than one hundred missionaries and other leading Christian workers came together; a very largely attended public meeting in the great Dharamtallah Street Methodist church; a Bengalee meeting in the Union church; and two or three workers' meetings as well.

At one of these workers' meetings "the United Society for India, Burmah, and Ceylon" was launched. It has an extensive name, but not a bit too extensive for the work it has to do, for in its field are more than three hundred millions of people. God grant that it may be a great evangelizing force among these myriads.

One of the leaders in preparing for these meetings and in promoting with his whole soul the cause of Christian Endeavor in Calcutta is Rev. R. M. Julian, pastor of the leading Baptist church of Calcutta. This is the church which Carey founded, and in which he preached when living at Serampore. Mr. Julian was already president of the Calcutta Christian Endeavor Union, and, very naturally and wisely, was chosen the first president of the United Society with the long name.

He will put into the new office all the energy of an earnest nature and of an ardent Endeavorer, who has tried and tested the Society both in England and in India.

This United Society is well off in secretaries, too, for it has three of them, Mr. McGaw, the statistical secretary, of whom you have already heard; Mr. Thompson, of Calcutta, a most wide-awake Endeavorer, the recording secretary, who will also furnish headquarters for the literature; and Mr. Burges, the newly appointed Sunday-school secretary for India, who was elected field secretary.

No better choices could possibly have been made. Mr. Burges is as enthusiastic for Christian Endeavor as for Sunday-school work, "because it has done so much for me," he says.

He formed the first society in Wales; he was the Welsh delegate to the Boston Convention —many of you remember him; and he will put Welsh fervor, shrewdness, eloquence, and devotion into his work, I am sure.

The General Council or board of trustees, represents many denominations and all parts of India, and will do all that human instrumentality can do to advance the cause. The treasurer is the leading Christian business man of Calcutta, Mr. Robert Laidlaw, of the most widely known business firm of India; in fact, he is the John Wanamaker of India.

No less cordial than the other denominations, I am glad to tell you, are the Methodists of India, two or three of whom are numbered in the Council. The honored Bishop Thoburn made a most kind and hearty address at the mass-meeting in Calcutta, and Miss Maxey of the same mission, who is one of the Council, is a whole board of trustees in herself. Several native Christians are on the General Council, as is most appropriate, among them Mr. Banurji and Mr. Chatterji, of Calcutta. Mr. Banurji is a very prominent lawyer and orator, and is sometimes called the Chauncey Depew of India.

Scotland, Ireland, Mexico, and all other ambitious countries, if you are expecting the badge-banner in 1897 for proportionate increase, I advise you to keep your eye on the empire of India.

But in all seriousness, I greatly rejoice in the work of the past week, and thank God for it; for I believe it means not only annexing a new continent to Christian Endeavor, but opening up a new means of evangelization for myriads of people. Who can tell what results, in the providence of God, may flow from those quiet, Spirit-inspired business meetings? Pray for India, Christian Endeavorers, as you never did before, for an increasing host of your Endeavor brothers and sisters will live in that great triangle between the salt seas.

XXXI

IN THE SOUTHERN EMPIRE

Southern India is an empire by itself, largely cut off, by language and difficulties of communication, from northern India. Christian Endeavor has a large domain here in the south, a domain which Rev. W. I. Chamberlain began to conquer some years ago with the help of friends in the Arcot and the Madura missions; a domain where some of the brightest victories of the future for Christ and Christian Endeavor of all kinds, I believe, will be won.

It is a four days' journey by water from Calcutta to Madras, down the treacherous Hooghly, one of the estuaries of the Ganges, and a river on whose shifting sand-bars two great steamers have recently been wrecked; then down the Bay of Bengal for seven hundred miles more.

Bright and early—or, rather, it was early and not bright, for it was scarcely dawn—the Malta cast anchor in Madras harbor. At the same moment Dr. Jacob Chamberlain appeared on her deck to welcome me and take me ashore. (By the way, let me ask you in parenthesis whether you have read Dr. Chamberlain's new book of fascinating missionary stories, "In the

Tiger Jungle"? If you have not, you have a treat before you.)

Soon we got into a big, flexible surf-boat, whose planks were tied together with rope and calked with hemp, since no ordinary boat can stand the fierce surf of Madras harbor. When we came near shore, the naked boatmen jumped over into the water, and formed a chair of their hands. In the old-fashioned way of my childhood, while we firmly grasped with each hand a sweaty, greasy black shoulder, we were borne to the strand.

Mr. David McConaughy's pleasant house was mine for the day—the same David McConaughy who is famous in Y. M. C. A. circles all over the world, and is doing a noble work for the young men of India. You will be glad to know that the corner-stone for the new Y. M. C. A. building, to which Hon. John Wanamaker has given $30,000, has just been laid.

Two services, one in the Y. M. C. A. hall and the other in the Free Church of Scotland, occupied the afternoon; and the next day, very early, I started for Tindivanum, where under the fostering care of Mr. and Mrs. Wyckoff Christian Endeavor has for some years had a home. Warm indeed was the greeting, with banners and music and a slow procession to the missionary bungalow. Over the gateway to the grounds was built a kind of welcome lodge; but

A SCENE IN INDIA

the banner which attracted most attention was a huge one stretching across the road and borne by four bearers, with the legend in great letters,—

> WELCOME TO REV. FATHER ENDEAVOR
> F. E. CLARK, D. D.

O Mr. Mills, Mr. Mills! does not your heart sometimes reproach you, even within the legislative halls of the Great and General Court of Massachusetts, for firing that atrocious joke heard round the world?

We had two delightful meetings in Tindivanum, and enjoyed the renewal of old friendships in the mission bungalow; and then pushed on the same night to Madura, the great mission station of the American Board in southern India.

This is one of the chief centres of Christian Endeavor in India, and more than a score of good societies are connected with this mission. The great West Gate church was filled on two occasions with dusky, earnest faces; and the next day I had the pleasure of speaking to the students of the famous college, theological seminary, and high school at Pasumalai, three miles distant.

Here Dr. Jones, an old friend of my schooldays, presides. He, by the way, is the first president of the new South India Christian Endeavor Union. In many directions he is doing a great work for the evangelization of India.

I wish I could introduce you personally to all the devoted missionaries of this mission, Mr. Vaughan and Mr. Holton and Dr. Van Allen and the "godly women not a few," as well as the native workers, who have done so much to establish Christian Endeavor under the shadow of the greatest, and in some respects the most magnificent, Hindu temple in the world.

The same day found me on the way to Battalagundu in a bullock bandy with Mr. Herrick, another of this mission band. A most enjoyable journey it was. At night we stopped in a deserted wayside bungalow to hold a Christian Endeavor meeting in a village a mile away. Close by was a grove of huge banyan-trees, and in the trees a whole colony of monkeys, big and little, old and young, sedate and frisky. They looked almost wise enough to form themselves into a society; only some of the younger members would have been too *active*, a fault not usually attributable to Christian Endeavorers. The way they jumped from tree to tree, and hung by their tails, and chased each other from branch to branch, was better than a whole zoölogical garden at home.

However, though no organization was effected in the banyan-tree, Mr. Samuel Joseph, my excellent interpreter, formed a society in this village of which I speak, and the next day at Battalagundu formed *five* others through the teachers and catechists there assembled.

XXXII

SWAMI VIVEKANANDA UPON HIS NATIVE HEATH

ONE of the Brahmans who made the greatest sensation while in America at the Parliament of Religions was the gorgeous and plausible Vivekananda. While I was in Madras he made his triumphal entrance to India. He deserves a chapter in this book.

A Hindu prophet is not always without honor in his own country. Swami Vivekananda has come back to India, has seen and conquered. Everywhere in southern India he has been received with more than royal acclaim. Triumphal arches have been erected; garlands innumerable have been hung upon his willing neck; his carriage has been unyoked from its horses and drawn by enthusiastic scholars and high dignitaries of the land, for is not he the great Brahman who has won the Western lands for Hinduism? Is not he the profound scholar, the eloquent orator, the astute diplomat, the master of assemblies, who, by waving his magic wand for a few months in Chicago, New York and London, has turned back the engulfing waters of Christianity, which threatened, only a few short years ago, to submerge the world—India included?

These are the ideas at least which the average Hindu seems to have imbibed, and we may be very sure that Vivekananda himself has done nothing to disabuse his countrymen of these notions. No wonder they call him "Swami" in their words, "God" Vivekananda.

But, though so exalted, this god is quite willing to be interviewed. He doubtless learned the trick when in America. Here are some choice extracts as they recently appeared in the Madras *Mail*.

"What was your experience of America, Swami?" asked the enterprising reporter.

"From first to last very good," answered Vivekananda. "With the exception of the missionaries and 'church women,' the Americans are most hospitable, kind-hearted, generous, and good-natured."

Naturally the reporter desired to know something of these "exceptions" who so fall below the average American, and so he asked, "Who are these church women that you speak of, Swami?"

Swami: "When a woman tries her best to find a husband she goes to all the bathing-places imaginable, and tries all sorts of tricks to catch a man. When she fails in her attempts, she becomes what they call in America an 'old maid,' and joins the church. Some of them become very 'churchy.' These church women are awful fanatics. They are under the thumb of the priests there. Between them and the priests they make a hell on earth. They make a mess of religion. With the exception of these the Americans are a very good people. They loved me so much. I loved them. I felt as though I was one of them."

After sounding the Swami on the interesting subject of "church women" the reporter asked him his idea concerning the Parliament of Religions. Here is Vivekananda's opinion.

"The Parliament of Religions, as it seems to me, was intended for a 'heathen show' before the world, but it turned out the heathen got the upper hand and made it a Christian show all around. So the Parliament of Religions was a failure from a Christian standpoint. But the Chicago parliament was a tremendous success for India and Indian thought. It helped on the tide of Vedanta which is flooding the world."

Having exhausted these American church women and the Parliament of Religions, the Swami adopts the rôle of prophet when asked, "What are the prospects of the spread of your mission in England?"

"There is every prospect," he replied, with jaunty confidence. "Before ten years elapse a vast majority of the English people will be Vedantins. There is a greater prospect of this in England than in America. You see Americans make a *fanfaronade* of everything, which is not the case with Englishmen."

Thus having predicted the complete triumph of Brahmanism in England, and that within the short space of one decade, he goes on to give an interesting view of the English character, which, on the whole, he esteems highly, as indeed is most fitting in a loyal subject of Queen Victoria. But this further estimate he confides to the willing ear of the reporter: " John Bull is rather a thick-headed gentleman to deal with. You must turn the screw and push the idea until it reaches his brain, but once there it does not get out. . . . To my astonishment many of my friends belong to the Church of England. I learn that these missionaries who howl (against me) come from the lowest classes in England. No Englishman will mix with them. Caste is as vigorous there as it is here, and the English churchman belongs to the class of gentlemen. Therefore I would give a word of advice to my countrymen; that is, not to take the least notice of all these vituperative missionaries, now that I have found out what they are. We have 'sized' them, as the Americans say. Non-recognition is the only attitude to assume toward them."

I might go on through many columns, quoting other choice bits from this sage of modern Brahmanism, but perhaps these are enough to show his braggadocio and deceit and his animus against missionaries and earnest Christians. This interview is surely sufficient to open the eyes of certain gullible Americans who petted and coddled him, and gave him the impression that they were so much superior to the despised missionaries and "church women" who "make a hell on earth."

That Vivekananda's return has made a deep impression upon certain portions of the Hindu community is certain. But I cannot find that the Christian community has been greatly affected by his bombastic claims. The arrival of Dr. John Henry Barrows in Madras at about the same time is a powerful antidote to Vivekananda's poison. Dr. Barrows is so uncompromising and outspoken in his defence of evangelical Christianity that he has won the hearts of all the missionaries and Christian workers. He has deeply impressed many Hindus as well, and when he leaves India he will doubtless be classed by Swami as a "low-caste American," perhaps not much better than the "church women" themselves.

XXXIII

OUR SIXTY DAYS IN INDIA

Our sixty days in India are nearly at an end, and this last week has been quite as interesting as any that has preceded. In the first place, on Monday, February 15, 1897, the representatives of South India ratified the United Society for India, Burmah, and Ceylon, so happily started at Calcutta a fortnight before, chose representatives for the council, and also formed a Christian Endeavor Union for South India, with Dr. Jones, of Madura, for president, and Rev. W. I. Chamberlain, of Vellore, for secretary.

Of Dr. Jones and his work I have already spoken, and Mr. Chamberlain is the same indefatigable worker who for years has led the Endeavor forces of the empire.

Then, when this new union was well launched, began a pleasant week of touring with Rev. R. Burges, our new field secretary, as I trust the Sunday-school Union, whose general secretary for India he is, will allow me to call him.

First we visited Coimbatoor, near the west coast, where the London Mission has a strong station. Here live Mr. Small and Rev. A. W.

Brough, whom I last met when he was a pastor in Maitland, Australia. In his beautifully decorated church there he greeted me in 1892, and now in another beautifully decorated church, seven thousand miles away, he has greeted me again. Here is a good Christian Endeavor society, and another in a Eurasian school supported by the generosity of Robert Stanes, Esq.

The same night we were again on the way, and the next afternoon found us at lovely Vellore, Rev. W. I. Chamberlain's home. Here a pleasant meeting was held, and another at Chittoor the next day. Chittoor is the mission station which is supported altogether by the Reformed (Dutch) Church Endeavorers of the United States. Most appropriate was it, then, that we should halt here for a half-day; and I am glad to congratulate the Endeavorers of this denomination on everything connected with *their own* station. In Mr. and Mrs. Beattie, the missionaries in charge, they have two devoted and efficient workers to sustain; the church is a noble one, one of the finest mission church buildings in India, and the girls' school is large and prosperous.

Rev. W. I. Chamberlain and his charming wife were formerly the missionaries at this station, but they have been transferred to Vellore. We all had our pictures taken by Mr.

Burges on the church tower,—three men on a tower,—with a great crowd of admiring Hindus looking on at the mysterious art of photography.

The next day was one of the most novel of the pilgrimage, for it was marked by the convention held with the village society of Yehamur, of the Arcot Mission.

A ride of twenty-one miles in an American buggy brought us near the village, and to a reception that was a reception. Half-a-dozen huge banners of welcome, a drum corps of a dozen drums of all possible and impossible shapes, a whole brass foundry of clashing cymbals, firecrackers, and other joyous expressions, greeted us. In triumph Mr. Burges and the missionaries, Mr. Beattie, Dr. Scudder,—in whose field is Yehamur,—and myself, were escorted across a wide field, through a heathen village. Here the drummers built grass fires, and heated their drums so that they gave forth a terrific din, enough to arouse the most hardened heathen.

At last the Christian part of the village was reached, and at the door of the roomy church the "tamasha" was resumed with redoubled vigor, until the not wholly imaginary headache of one of the party was pleaded as an excuse for silencing the hospitable noise.

Two afternoon meetings were held, but the great event was the evening service. Before the addresses we were all garlanded most profusely. Before the evening was over, I counted four heavy garlands of yellow flowers around my neck, one composed of six strings of flowers. A gorgeous bird of paradise, made of tinsel paper and perched on a flower-decorated stick, was thrust into my hand, and six limes were given me to hold. Pomegranates were given us, and Mr. Burges's weakness for bananas was recognized by a large bunch. An address of welcome in a beautiful sandalwood box and a lyric sung to a spirited native tune formed part of the exercises.

Modesty forbids me to quote the poem in full, but one verse ran in polite Oriental phrase as follows:—

"O Arcot Endeavorers, clap your hands enthusiastically,
Garland our Dr. Clark with flowers,
Sprinkle him with plenty of rose-water."

Suiting the action to the word, a swarthy Tamil brother deluged me with fragrant rose-water, and then proceeded to sprinkle liberally my friends on the platform, while the song went on uninterruptedly through fifteen or twenty verses.

But the best of "tamashas" must come to an end, as this one did. A long moonlight ride brought us to Dr. Scudder's hospitable bungalow, where we enjoyed two hours of sleep before taking the train for Madras at three in the morning.

The Madras Christian Endeavor meeting, held later in the day, was an encouraging and hopeful one, though the movement has as yet taken slight hold in that great city. The strong and brotherly address of Dr. Rudishill, of the Methodist Episcopal Church, would have done your hearts good in its outspoken, enthusiastic stand for our Christian Endeavor interdenominational fellowship.

This meeting was scarcely over before we were again upon the train, for an all night's ride to Madanapalle, where was established, you remember, the pioneer Christian Endeavor society in South India,—a society which for seven years has done splendid work.

Here live my dear friends, Dr. and Mrs. Jacob Chamberlain, and Rev. L. B. Chamberlain. Of the pleasures of these last two days before sailing for Africa I cannot begin to tell you, but I shall never forget them. I can only say that the first meeting was held near the station of Chinna Tippusamudram, under the auspices of the vigorous senior society of Madanapalle. Here was organized a society which rejoices in having a record-breaking name for length. Other meetings in Madanapalle revealed the grasp of Christian Endeavor in this, one of its earliest strongholds of India.

Now my sixty days in India are numbered. I sail this afternoon for Natal, South Africa, a twenty-three days' voyage in a small coolie emigrant steamer. I thank God for these sixty days. I am leaving this great continent, encouraged beyond measure concerning the future of Christian Endeavor in India and the Society's adaptability to this country. These days have been among the most busy and most memorable of my life. If I have given any of my readers the impression that this has been one long picnic, let me remind them that into these sixty days have been crowded eighty-one addresses to people who speak seven different languages, and more than six thousand miles of travel, and that nearly one-half of the nights have been spent on the rail. A picnic! "That is no name for it." A sixty days' picnic is not to be compared with a sixty days' tour among the Christian Endeavorers of India.

XXXIV

A SKY PILOT ON A COOLIE SHIP

For the sake of the landsmen among my readers,—and I suppose they are in a decided majority,—let me first introduce them both to the sky pilot and to the coolie ship.

The "sky pilot" is a certain individual of whom they have heard before, who is taking a long journey for the advancement of Christian Endeavor interests, from India's coral strand to Afric's sunny fountains. By sailors in general he and all his brothers of the ministerial calling are designated as "sky pilots," in good-natured contempt, I suppose, for their presumed ignorance of sublunary things in general, and of nautical matters in particular. But this sky pilot, at least, is very willing to accept the title, and only hopes that he may be able to live up to it, and pilot some human craft to the skies.

The coolie ship is the nearest approach to the old-fashioned "slaver" that sails the seas to-day. This particular ship, the good Congella, carries indentured coolies, the lowest class of Hindu laborers, from Madras to Natal. Though more like the old-fashioned slave-ship than any other afloat, it is, thank fortune, far removed from that abomination of desolation; for the Natal government exercises a paternal solicitude for its emigrants, and, though they are going to a new continent to work hard on plantations, they are going of their own free will, and in the hope of bettering their poor fortunes. The government itself imports them, as they are better laborers than the native Zulus, guarantees them their wages, and agrees to take them back to India at the end of five years if they wish to go. Moreover, this paternal government is so very paternal that it vaccinates its future citizens, and segregates them for a week before sailing, to make sure that they start with no contagious disease; then burns all their clothing, to make certain that there go aboard as few as possible unseen passengers, minute stowaways that do not appear in the ship's manifest.

Then it gives to each future citizen, men and women alike, impartially, a strip of white cotton cloth, while all that the children need is a tow string to fasten on the pieces of tin bearing their numbers, a smile, and, if they can afford it, a necklace of beads. Then it puts them aboard the steamer, with sufficient rice and pumpkins and other "curry stuff" to last for three weeks and two days, with a supply of tobacco also; for I am sorry to say that all the future citizens, even down to the four-year-old toddler, are addicted to the weed.

Moreover, the paternal government of Natal is so paternal that it dooms us all, coolies and sky pilot alike, to twenty-three days at sea, though the voyage could easily be made in eighteen, lest we carry some dire disease to the Natalese. The reasoning seems to be: In twenty-three days the disease, whatever it is, will have time to run its course, and the passengers will either be all well or all dead, and in neither case can they contaminate us.

To be sure, it is not exactly a pleasant thought that one is doomed to imprisonment for twenty-three days on a possible pest-ship without any possibility of a reprieve; but then the sky pilot ought not to complain, for it is by special favor, as it were, that he is allowed to make one of this happy family. He is the only white passenger, and, though he pays more than one hundred dollars for his accommodations and disaccommodations, he came near being refused altogether by the paternal government. For has he not been wandering all over India? Has he been segregated for a week? Will he allow his clothing to be burned? "No, indeed," he says; "they are poor things, sir, but mine own." So the "protector" of the paternal government deliberates over his case, shakes his head wisely, but at length allows him to go aboard with his ticket indorsed, "It is my opinion that Rev. —— can embark without danger to the coolies."

Somehow the sky pilot had never thought of it in that light before, and had, in his Anglo-Saxon pride of cleanliness, supposed that he was the one in danger of contamination; but pride must ever have its fall and self-conceit its Waterloo.

But now we have been at sea seventeen days, and the sky pilot has had a chance to learn something about his fellow-passengers. Perhaps you would like to share his observations. We are, to all intents and purposes, in a little world by ourselves. There is no possible communication, except with the fishes below and the blessed angels above. For twenty-three days we are cut off from all commerce with our kind. No telegrams, no penny-post, no express package, can reach our floating island. Europe may be submerged by a tidal wave; Lord Salisbury may have been induced to say something decisive on the Eastern question, though I very much doubt it; America may have been frozen stiff in a March blizzard, who knows? We certainly do not, for was not a new president to have been inaugurated on the fourth of March, now eleven days ago? and no news thereof has reached our distant planet.

But now for the population of this little

iron asteroid,—our esteemed fellow-passengers. There are four hundred of them, and they lie strewn thickly over the decks by day and the hold by night, so thickly that the sky pilot has to pick his way gingerly whenever he takes his walks abroad, lest he step on an outstretched finger or toe, or a coolie baby. This somewhat limits his exercise, for he has no desire, like the conquerors of old, to tread on human necks.

The following characteristics he has noticed in his fellow-passengers. They love a little brief authority. Some of them have a letter S on their arms to show that they are sirdars. Under them are the topas, not jaspers or emeralds, but topas, whose duty is to sweep the decks, and they are marked with a "T." How the sirdars do like to order about the topas! How they yank them by the ear, and pull them by the hair, when they do not do their work satisfactorily! O thou autocratic sirdar, type of so many minds in many larger kingdoms, whose heads are turned by a little sudden rise in power and dignity, teach us all, by thy absurd airs, lessons of humility and lowliness.

Many of my fellow-passengers are much given to ornaments. To be sure, most of them are absurdly poor, a quarter of an anna (one-half a cent) being more than the united cash possessions of some whole families; but these same families indulge in many brass bangles and ornaments. For instance, in each ear of one of my fellow-passengers I counted four earrings; in her nose were three more ornaments, one on each side and one depending from the cartilaginous division in the middle. Three of her toes also sported a heavy pewter ring each, while her ankles and wrists jingled with many bracelets. The total money value of the whole ornamental outfit might possibly be five cents; but I noticed that because of them she put on many airs, and seemed to consider herself quite superior to unadorned females.

In the eyes of the angels, the sky pilot said to himself, is it not possible that the crowns of royalty and the coronets of nobility and the diamonds of the rich, which are the occasion of so much exclusiveness on the one side and envy on the other, are of no more value than this poor coolie's baubles?

Again, my fellow-passengers have many habits that offend a squeamish stomach and a sensitive soul. They are quarrelsome, and sometimes must be tied to the rail for fighting. They eat more like pigs at a trough than like human beings. Fingers, in their estimation, were evidently made long before spoons and forks. They have never discovered the use of a pocket-handkerchief, and the "Madras hunt" is constantly in progress on deck.

But from twenty-three days amid these unpleasant sights and sounds, and worse smells, the sky pilot is determined to learn a lesson of tolerance and humility; for is there not high authority for the saying, "In many things we offend all"? Sky pilot, look to thyself. The coolies are not the only ones who have joints in their armor and flies in their ointment.

XXXV

TWENTY-THREE DAYS AT SEA AND SOME REFLECTIONS

Twenty-three days at sea, the only white passenger on a crowded ship, gives one time for many reflections. I hope I have not entirely wasted my time; and, if you do not object, my dear fellow travellers, I will share some of my thoughts with you; though, as I know the antipathy of most mortals to moral reflections, and the inconsiderateness of many moral reflectors, I will try not to bore you.

In the first place, we are all here together on this ship for better or worse for three and twenty days. There is no getting off the ship. There is no calling at any island or port on the way. Here we are, and here we must stay for three weeks and two days, according to the decree of the Natal government, to give any infectious disease we may have brought from India time to show itself. If the poorest coolie should be taken with the cholera, we should all be involved in a common danger. If the smallest little naked child, kicking about on the decks, should have the smallpox, we should all be quarantined after arrival, perhaps for weeks. I was obliged to sign a contract before coming on board, saying that I would submit, if necessary, to the same quarantine "as the other emigrants" on the bluff at Durban.

What is this but saying, as the Scripture saith, "If one member suffer, all the members suffer with it"? How admirable an illustration for good-citizenship committees! We as a nation are all metaphorically "in the same boat," as I am actually with these four hundred coolies. If one poor emigrant to America introduces moral contagion, the whole country suffers more or less contamination. The true patriot is the one who tries to stop the disease before the whole body politic is sick and sore.

Again, I have often reflected that there is just one man on board who knows the way over this interminable waste of waters. Even the first mate at the beginning of the voyage did not know the course we should take. When I asked him on the first day out, he told me he could not tell how "the old man," as he called the captain, had decided to go.

But the captain knew. He had studied the charts, and knew how the currents set at this time of year, and when the trade-winds would be felt, and where good weather might be expected; and so he steered cautiously around Ceylon, skirted the Maldive Islands, struck boldly across the Indian Ocean, took the narrow channel between bold Comoro and Johanna off the coast of Madagascar, and then steamed down the middle of the great Mozambique Channel to Durban. I am glad he knows the way. It makes very little difference whether I do or not. He directs the ship.

I like to think of the "Captain of our salvation" sometimes as a ship-captain rather than as a military captain. He knows the way, and he steers my bark. The captain of our steamer knows, every day at noon, after he has "taken the sun," just where we are, even within a mile; and I have faith to believe that he will find the little dent on the African coast called Durban harbor, after crossing this great and wide sea, and will take me in safety across the bar. I have the same faith, infinitely increased, in the great Captain, and when each night comes I can peacefully go to sleep. He is at the helm. He knows the safe harbor at the end. He will take me across the bar.

I have spoken of the ocean currents. They are a great factor on this voyage. Sometimes they are against us, retarding our speed from two to four knots an hour; sometimes, and more often, for our captain knows where they run and how to take advantage of them, they are with us, helping our speed just as much. They are like vast rivers, deeper and wider and stronger than any Mississippi or Amazon, flowing through the midst of the ocean.

So in all our lives are such strong, oversweeping currents of passion, of circumstance, of environment, of prejudice. They are unseen of men, but none the less real and potent. Our Captain, too, knows where these life-currents run; and, if we allow our lives to be guided by him, he will so steer our course that all these currents will be a help, not a hindrance. Even when they seem most adverse for a time, we can make head against them if we will, as our iron steamer with its thousand-horse-power engine makes head against the adverse current of the Indian Ocean.

Once more, the end of the voyage is always in mind, a joyful anticipation. What would induce a landsman with a quiet, comfortable home to leave it, and endure the miseries of seasickness twenty-three days on a coolie ship with its filth and its indifferent food, its lukewarm water, its cockroaches, its other vermin that it is still less proper to mention in polite society, and its unutterable smells? What would induce one to do this? Why, the end in view, to be sure, would induce you or me or any of us to take the voyage. If it was our duty and we could succeed in planting Christian Endeavor a little more firmly in the great African continent, there are few of us who would not start to-morrow. Many times I have thought of South Africa and the work there, and then of the home-going afterward; and almost every hour has been brightened by present work and pleasant anticipations.

Why should we not brighten our long earthly journey far more than we do with delightful anticipations of the journey's end, and of the work and the home that await us?

XXXVI

AFRICA AT LAST

HERE we are, at last, my dear fellow travellers, in South Africa, the land of our hopes and anticipations for many a long week. A wonderful country is Natal, with its lovely, rolling hills, clothed in living green, its deep cañons, its vast table-lands dotted with the cattle from a thousand hillsides; a country of marvellous resources, of brilliant promise, of a checkered and blood-stained history, but of a glorious future, I believe.

Christian Endeavor, too, at least in Natal and the Transvaal, is mostly in the future, and these are the days of beginnings.

I landed in Durban, being set free from the prison pest-house of the emigrant steamer on the twenty-third of March; and that same evening I attended a Christian Endeavor meeting in the Baptist church of Pastor Rose, who has the only living Young People's society in the city, though there are two Juniors. There has been a sad mortality among the societies in Durban, something like the rinderpest among the cattle in the Transvaal.

I do not know what the reason is, unless it

may be due to the bacillus "amusement" or "entertainment"; but certain it is that in no other part of the world have there been so many deaths in the Christian Endeavor family. In fact, it is usually the rarest thing in the world to hear of the death of a society once fairly established.

I especially enjoyed a visit of three hours (which was all the many meetings in Durban allowed) to Amanzimtote, one of the stations of the American Board's Zulu mission. First an hour in the train, then three hours in a wagon drawn by four oxen, and then the white buildings and schoolhouses of the Adams mission station at Amanzimtote came in sight.

I should like to describe this work at length, and tell you about all these devoted workers; but space forbids. I can assure you there is no more heroic, self-sacrificing, noble body of mission workers in all the world; and within a very few weeks the prayers of scores of years have been answered, and the labors of three-quarters of a century rewarded, by the most remarkable outpouring of God's Spirit that this, or, perhaps, any other station has ever known.

As I write, meetings of wonderful power are held daily. They extend into the night, and sometimes last all night; the sons and the daughters are prophesying, and the Zulu

Christians are bowed down with a sense of their sin like reeds in the river by the onrushing current.

One of the devoted missionaries here, the Rev. Charles N. Ransom, has been the superintendent of Christian Endeavor in South Africa for seven years. He has been instant in season and out of season. I dimly suspect that he seems to some of the brethren like a Christian Endeavor crank, who has been trying to introduce some newfangled Yankee religious patent.

To me, if he will forgive the illustration, he seems more like a twenty-four ox team, such as I have often seen on the roads of South Africa, striving to drag the wagon Christian Endeavor over the heavy roads and up the steep hills of indifference that always oppose a new idea.

In Pietermaritzburg, the capital of the colony, are two good Endeavor societies, one in the Congregational, the other in the Baptist, church; and the meetings here, though somewhat interfered with by deluges of rain (real tropical cloudbursts), were large and full of spiritual power. The chain of prayer and the warm evangelistic spirit made me feel that I was indeed at home. Here live Rev. Walter Searle and his gifted wife, both of whom are so well known by their writings in connection with the Keswick movement. Here, too, I was the guest of Mr. Henry Bale, a member of the

Natal Parliament, and one of the leading citizens in the colony, who has been induced to open his beautiful home most hospitably, and especially to homeless young men, by reading the books of "Pansy," an author whom he greatly admires. How far these books have carried the spirit of their author, and how these pansies bloom in far-away lands!

In Ladysmith we had two meetings, the second one in the pretty town hall; and the next day I pushed on across the uplands of the Transvaal to Johannesburg, one of the modern wonders of the world; a city of more than a hundred thousand inhabitants, which has been waved into existence in ten years by the magic wand of gold.

We are reminded constantly that things are in a very unsettled and perilous state here, and that a revolution may set in at any moment. On the boarders of the Transvaal I was stopped, and my passport demanded, and very properly, owing to the excited state of feeling in this republic. On arriving, I was interviewed by a reporter of *The Star*, or rather of *The Comet*, for the day before, *The Star*, an independent newspaper, had been suspended for three months by President Kruger. *The Comet* then appeared, explaining that *The Star* had disappeared into space for three months, but *The Comet*, another of the heavenly bodies, with a solid head and a frightful tail, had taken its place.

Now, as I write these last words, comes the glad news from home of the meetings on Christian Endeavor Day, and of the deepening of the spiritual life of so many in connection with Mr. Meyer's visit to America. It is but a repetition of the good news that has come to me from many a land during the past year. North America and South Africa can join hands in this. Anglo-Saxon Christians and Zulu Christians have alike shared the blessing. Dear Endeavorer, you who read these words, has this blessing untold come into your individual life? If not, why not?

XXXVII

THE AFRICAN AT HOME

The African at home is a bright, good-natured, cheerful, musical, happy-go-lucky, improvident, impulsive, faithful fellow.

To be sure, there are Africans and Africans. They speak many languages and occupy widely separated sections of a vast continent, but they have many characteristics in common. It must also be said that there is a great difference between the "raw Kaffir" in his kraal and the civilized Christian native. But let us look at him as we find him, in a state of nature and also in a state of grace. The Zulu undoubtedly represents the finest race of Africans physically and mentally. He has impressed his characteristics upon many other races whom he has conquered, while he in turn has been conquered by the English and the Dutch and—the Maxim gun.

As you see the Zulu in the streets of Durban, for instance, he strikes you as the jolliest, lightest-hearted individual in existence. He has a superabundance of life and vitality. He dances and sings upon the street-corner. When he draws you in the jinrikisha, he prances and

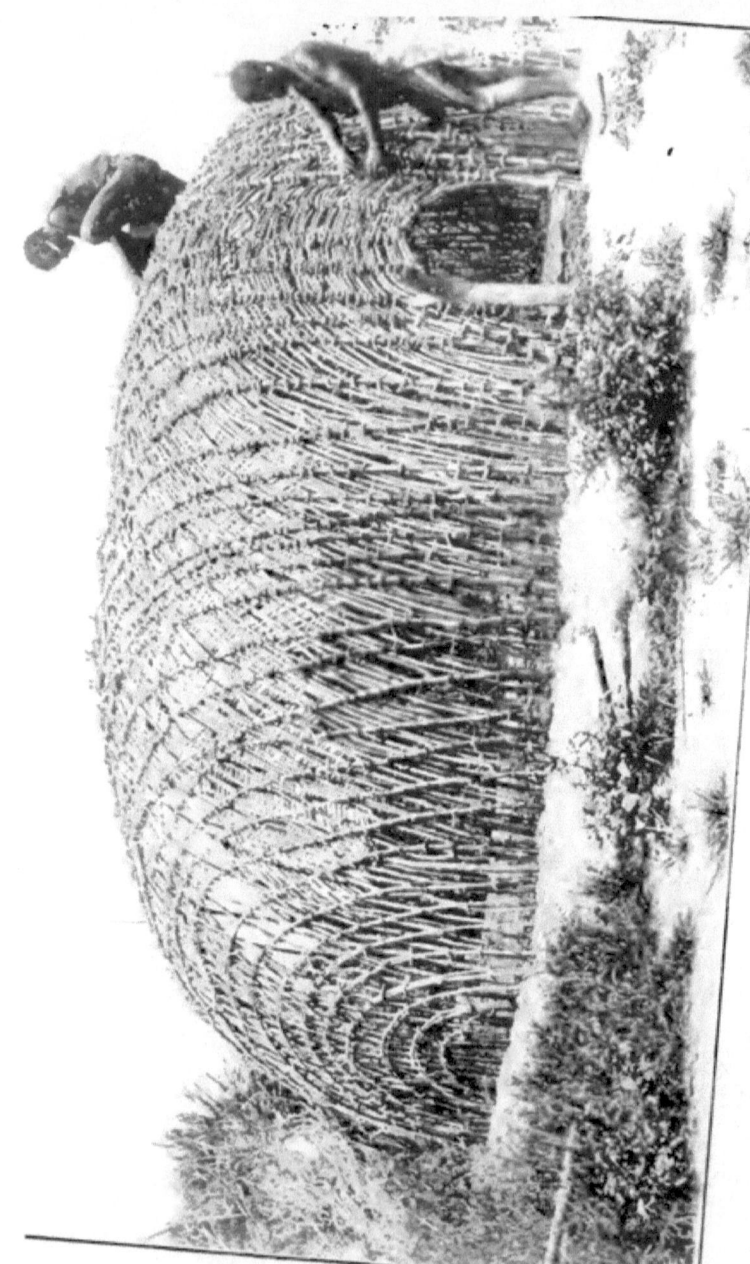

AN AFRICAN KRAAL

gallops and puffs and snorts like a steam-engine; and "choo, choo, choos" as if he were a veritable locomotive. Life seems to be one prolonged holiday to him if only he can get enough "mealies" (Indian corn) and sweet potatoes to eat.

In the most fantastic and grotesque garbs does he dress. You will see him in all soberness marching down the principal street of Durban with a battered tall silk hat rakishly perched on one side of his head, and his nether extremities clad in a gorgeous blanket of as many colors as Joseph's traditional coat. Or you will see him arrayed chiefly in beads; a bead apron tied about his loins, a heavy chain of beads about his neck, a huge coil of beads bound about his forehead, great bead earrings in his ears, bracelets and anklets of the same, and a pair of big bead goggles, with no glasses in them, over his eyes.

Many of the "'rickshaw" men wear huge ostrich plumes as tall as a drum-major's, while others bind a pair of great horns from some defunct steer upon their heads, and go galloping gayly off with their big baby-carriages, containing one or two men, as if they were mere children. When such an apparition appears upon the street, you feel inclined to look at his feet to see whether he has hoofs as well as horns.

Our African at home lives in a grass or mud

hut, of a circular shape and some fifteen or twenty feet in diameter. The floor is made of hard pounded mud, and in the middle is a mud fireplace, from which the smoke curls up through a hole in the roof. He requires very little furniture, for he squats on the floor, and rolls himself up in his blanket at night, with his head on a curved wooden block in lieu of a pillow.

I have crawled into several of these kraal huts, and can say from experience that loftiness must be abased, and that "topknot" must come down, before one can enter these straight and narrow doorways.

If our Zulu is well-to-do, he has three or four or even a dozen or more huts, in each one of which a dusky wife presides and rears her own brood of pickaninnies. Moreover, the wives must earn their husband's bread, while the lord of creation sits lazily by, engaged in the arduous operation of smoking a pipe or a cigar. A cigar, by the way, he usually puts into his mouth fire end first, so as to get the benefit of all the smoke.

Since the women do the work, it comes about that they are valuable property in Zululand, and a man is accounted a citizen of substance and weight according to the number of his wives. Instead of giving a dowry, as do the fathers of the countries where effete Western civilization prevails, the would-be husband pays the father roundly for his daughter, a likely young girl bringing from twelve to twenty cows, while, if the father is a chief, or head man, he will not part with his daughter for less than thirty cows.

"Revolting!" do you say? "A disgusting, degrading habit"? But how much worse are these open bargains than the marriages for convenience or for fortune, or the sale of American beauty for an English coronet? I venture to say there is quite as much love among the Kaffirs of the kraals, who buy their wives for a dozen cows, as among the British or American youth who find it convenient to marry a girl with a cool hundred thousand in the bank.

I must say that it appeared to me that the natives were hardly treated in Africa; far more roughly on their native soil than in America, the land of their forced adoption.

For instance, in all South Africa there is a curfew law which obliges the African, but not the European, to be at home before nine o'clock in the evening; otherwise, he is liable to arrest and imprisonment. This law is said to be most beneficial, but it surely bears hard upon the poor fellow who may be going home from a religious meeting, or is called to see a sick friend, and has not reached home before the stroke of nine.

To be sure, a pass from his master or pastor may save him from arrest, if he has been thoughtful enough to provide himself with one. But change places with the Zulu, my pale-faced brother, and consider how you would like to have some lordly black man regulate your hours of going or coming.

Moreover, in many parts of South Africa, if not in all, the natives are not allowed to walk upon the sidewalks, or to ride in the street-cars; and, if they wish to go by rail, they cannot go in first or second class cars, but must herd together in filthy third or fourth class carriages. On some of the farms they are treated with abominable cruelty, and in many parts of the continent a white man would never be brought to book for killing a "nigger."

In short, the black man in his own land has few rights which the white man is bound to respect; and there is no room on African soil for the doctrine that all men were created free and equal.

Bad as may be the treatment of the black man in some other parts of the world, there is no place where he is so shamefully treated as in the land of his birth, the land of which he has been largely despoiled.

But there is a brighter side to this picture. There are many earnest Christian people who feel these wrongs and are trying to right them.

Many churches and schools have been established for the natives, which are doing a splendid work. Almost all denominations of Christians are alive to the importance of the work among the Africans. Better than all else, in no part of the world, perhaps, is the Spirit of God working more wonderfully than in the American Zulu mission of Natal. For sixty years faithful missionaries of the cross have been laboring in this field, often amid much discouragement and with small results; but within a twelvemonth a change has come, the flood-gates have been opened and the showers of grace have followed the drops of divine favor.

Heart-searchings and confessions began among the Christians. Especially in the mission schools for young men and women did the work of grace become manifest.

Meetings which began at seven o'clock in the evening were continued until three o'clock in the morning, and sometimes until the gray dawn appeared in the eastern sky, and even then it was with difficulty that the missionaries could persuade the penitent young souls to go to their homes and get a little rest before beginning the work of another day.

"The sons and the daughters prophesied," and scores and hundreds gave their hearts to Christ. The work spread from mission station to mission station; the missionaries themselves were greatly moved to a new consecration, and preached and labored with hopefulness and joy and success such as they had never known before.

As I write, the good work is still going on with ever increasing power. May it spread throughout all the land till darkest Africa becomes bright.

XXXVIII

THE TWO REPUBLICS OF THE SOUTHERN CROSS

Two little republics under the Southern Cross have attracted more than their fair share of the world's attention during the last twelve months. These two States are the South African Republic, or the Transvaal, as the land across the river Vaal is indifferently called, and the Orange Free State, to the south of the Transvaal, which took its name from valiant William of Orange, and in honor of its name covers its coat of arms with fruitful orange-trees in full bearing.

The South African Republic, it is true, has rather monopolized the world's attention, to the exclusion of its smaller sister. Telegraph wires and cables have been kept hot with news more or less (usually less) authentic, which would have been exceedingly important if true. Its old Dutch president, Johannes Stephanos Paul Kruger, has been treated by reporters and newspaper correspondents as though he was one of the world's great potentates—as indeed he is if a man's power is measured by the amount of commotion he is able to make in the cabinet councils of the nations. His goings out and his comings in have been recorded, his downsittings and his uprisings, and when he sneezes it is almost as though Queen Victoria herself had taken cold.

One of the anomalous things of present-day politics is the power which this old, unlettered Boer has been able to exert in the world. I use these adjectives with the utmost respect, simply in the interests of accuracy, for with all his power and deserved influence, the old ruler of the Transvaal is, from the scholar's ordinary standpoint, one of the most ignorant men who ever sat in a presidential chair. There is but one book which he can read, and that is the Bible. But, it may be asked, how does it happen that if he can read one book he cannot read all books? The explanation given in the Transvaal is that, being gifted with a remarkably tenacious memory, he has, from constantly hearing the Bible read in public from his boyhood up, committed all of its more familiar passages to heart; so that when he takes up a copy of the Scriptures and his eye lights upon a well-known verse, he can go on indefinitely from memory.

Nor can this modern South African Colossus write any better than he can read. To be sure, he can sign his name to public documents, but in somewhat the same way that Osman the Great, the founder and first sultan of the

Osmanli Turks, used to sign his name to public documents—by dipping his hand in a saucer of ink and spreading it out on the paper, thus literally making his *sign manual*. Not that President Kruger has not got beyond Osman the First, for he can guide the quill sufficiently to sign his name to papers of state; but to *write* one of those papers, or even an ordinary letter, with his own hand, would be quite beyond his powers, is the story often told in Pretoria. And yet should I leave the impression with my readers that he was simply an ignorant old Boer, it would be a very false impression. From the scholar's standpoint, possibly he is that, but from the standpoint of the politician and man of affairs he is one of the shrewd great men of the time. If he cannot write a state document, he can dictate one. He knows what is in every one that he signs, and his native shrewdness enables him to get the better of far more scholarly rulers of mightier realms than his when the interests of his "poor burghers," as he pathetically calls them, are concerned.

To call him the Lincoln of South Africa is altogether extravagant praise. He has none of the broad, far-seeing, statesmanlike views of Lincoln; his integrity is far from spotless if common report is not utterly libellous; and he has little of the brilliant eloquence that made possible a Gettysburg oration. But he is like Lincoln in this important respect—he knows the common people thoroughly and accurately. He sprang from them; he is one of them. With all his wealth and power, he has never set himself above them. When I called upon him in Pretoria a few weeks ago a young Boer farmer was sitting upon the veranda of the presidential mansion, which, by the way, is a very unpretentious cottage. The young farmer was collarless and dirty, and his mud-splashed brogans showed that he was a son of the soil; but he evidently felt that there was nothing in his appearance or his clothes which should debar him from a familiar interview with his president. The president, too, seemed to be of the same opinion, and they chatted together as unconstrainedly as any two cronies, while the old *vrow* Madam Kruger, sitting near by, placidly knit her heavy woollen stockings like any venerable housewife of the Transvaal.

This is the secret of the power of the President of the South African Republic. He is one of the people—a representative Boer; a typical Dutch farmer, with all the limitations and all the sturdiness, conservatism, strong religious feeling, and native common sense of his race developed in an unusual degree. These qualities, too, characteristic in a greater or less degree of the Boers as a race, account for the prominence of their remote little republic among the greater nations of the world. Here is a new race, a distinct type of mankind, a unique people that has found its home in the heart of South Africa. Except in the matter of language, they are no more Dutch than they are French or Scotch. In fact, many of them dislike and distrust the Holland Dutch more than they do the English themselves. A large admixture of French Huguenot blood flows in the veins of many of them, and many families have French names, corrupted often into their Dutch equivalents.

In religion the people are far more like the Scotch Covenanters of two centuries ago than like the modern rationalistic, sacerdotal church of Holland. In fact, so alarmed were the Boers some seventy-five years ago at the spread of rationalistic formalism in their nation that they sent to Scotland for some young ministers who were sound in the faith. Among those who responded to the call was Andrew Murray, the father of the Andrew Murray of the present day—that prince of mystics whose books are read by the whole Christian world. This young Scotchman and his descendants and a few others of his stamp have wonderfully moulded the religious life of the two republics, and have imparted a sturdy, God-fearing, Bible-loving character to all their inhabitants.

The Puritan type of character is very strongly developed among the Dutch Boers, and this it is which the Rt. Hon. Joseph Chamberlain must reckon with in dealing with that handful of Dutch farmers that inhabit the Transvaal. I do not mean to aver that the Boers are either as intelligent or as morally spotless as the Pilgrim fathers; and it is very sure that they are not actuated by as lofty religious motives, nor have they been tested by such stern experience as were the *Mayflower's* passengers and their descendants. But they certainly are imbued with the Puritan spirit, with many of its excellencies as well as many of its defects, and this spirit makes them a people to be reckoned with by the mightiest of nations.

Moreover, it must be borne in mind that they look upon the recent hordes of British and Americans and Germans—in fact, Uitlanders generally—as interlopers and usurpers, and that they have some reason for this opinion. Until gold was discovered on the Rand no one cared for the Transvaal. The Boers might keep it to themselves for all England cared. Who wished for a huge barren sheep-farm where the prickly-pear was the only thing that really seemed to thrive? Especially undesirable was a great tract of ground where the city of Johannesburg now stands. It was so exceedingly barren that scarcely could the hardy African sheep find anything to nibble. On one side was the farm of the Bramble Fountain, on the other, a mile away, the farm of the Thorn Fountain. Their very names were unpromising and hopeless. But one fine morning pay streaks of gold were found on the ridge of land that connected the Bramble Fountain with the Thorn Fountain, and from that moment the Transvaal was a different place. For weal or woe the old chapter of its poverty stricken history was closed and a new Golconda-like chapter was opened, and all eyes were dazzled with visions of unbounded wealth.

Then adventurers poured in from all quarters of the globe—British and German, French and Dutch, American and Portuguese. The land which Great Britain would scarcely take as a gift a few years before was the prize of many covetous eyes. The exchequer which had been as bare as Mother Hubbard's cupboard was soon almost bursting with golden guineas. Beggars suddenly became choosers of champagne and truffles, and the poor who walked yesterday were riding in their chaises to-day.

Upon the wretched soil of the farms of the Thorn Fountain and the Bramble Fountain arose the stately city of Johannesburg, with its tall brick buildings, its churches, its big hotels, its shops resplendent with plate glass, its electric tramways, its gambling-hells and gin-palaces. In ten years the desert blossomed, not with the rose—nothing so innocent and fragrant as that—but it did blossom into a great "rustling," bustling, busy, wicked city of a hundred thousand inhabitants. The mines, which now almost surround the city, continued to pour out their almost unbounded stores of yellow metal. Some of them pay 120 per cent a year on the capital invested. New mines were constantly opened up, some of them as valuable as the great originals, others of them utterly worthless. Companies were floated with enormous capital, many of them worth about as much as the paper on which the stock certificates were printed. Speculation grew wild and rampant. Men lost their heads and women lost fortunes.

Kimberley, which in the early days of its diamond mines had passed through a similar era of wild excitement, emptied its adventurers into this new Golconda. Barney Barnato, who, if general rumor is to be believed, laid the foundation of his colossal fortune in illicit diamond-buying at Kimberley—which means buying diamonds for a song of natives and others who had stolen them—emigrated to Johannesburg and became the mighty moneyed magnate of the Transvaal. His partner in the diamond business, Cecil Rhodes, while holding on to his diamond mines, also acquired large interests in Johannesburg, and the little Jew and the big

Englishman were followed by a horde of adventurers, little and big, all on one thing intent, and that the putting the yellow money of the Transvaal in their purses.

It can be imagined that this golden stream which began to flow so suddenly and so unstintedly should at its flood have swept many an otherwise stable character off its foundation. Foreigners were in possession of the mines. Almost before the Boers had rubbed open their drowsy eyelids to see what had happened to their poverty-stricken country, every mine worth opening had been claimed by these Egyptians, the Uitlanders, and nothing remained to the original inhabitants of the Promised Land but to spoil the Egyptians. This, if the Egyptians are to be believed, they at once proceeded to do. Large sums were charged for all sorts of "concessions." Monopolies were sold to the highest bidder. Dynamite, a necessity in goldmining operations, was taxed till it was almost ready to explode from sheer indignation. An iniquitous company from Holland built the railway which quickly connected the gold-fields with the rest of the world, and immensely overcharged its patrons for transportation.

There is no doubt that this sudden rise of the golden flood until it submerged the whole land left behind much foul sediment of corruption and bribery in high places and in low.

One of the many stories current in Pretoria, the capital of the Transvaal, relates to the "American spider." Now the American spider, it must be understood, spins no film and weaves no web; it is simply an inoffensive four-wheeled vehicle of light construction, imported from America and much in vogue in South Africa, the vehicle which we should call a buggy.

On one occasion a number of the burghers who constitute the Volksraad, or lower house of legislature, voted for a measure which greatly enriched one of their number, whereupon the next morning each one found at his door a brand-new American "spider," shining in its unmarred paint and varnish.

When the Volksraad assembled, one of the unbribed minority was noticed clutching in an insane way at imaginary insects on the wall and on the desks of the house of assembly. His queer antics and unsuccessful grabbings after nothing naturally attracted attention, and when asked by his brotherly legislators, who thought he might be seeing reptiles rather than insects, what he was doing, he replied that he was "only trying to catch a spider." Whenever the presenter of the "spiders" appears upon the streets to-day, he is greeted by the malicious small boy with cries of "Spider!" "Spider!" "How much are American spiders?"

Those who think they know, say that even

the gray and grizzled president himself has fallen from grace; that, devoutly religious as he undoubtedly was a score of years ago and as he now is in all outward forms and ceremonies, he is not above allowing a gift to influence his decision, and that through thus spoiling the Egyptians in various ways he has become enormously wealthy.

However that may be, it is no doubt true that up to the time of the foolish and inexcusable Jameson raid, the Uitlanders had the grievances largely on their side. But this disastrous raid utterly turned the balances the other way, until the Uitlanders' side kicked the beam.

At once public opinion, justice, and the balance of righteousness shifted to the other side; and the Uitlanders and their cause received a blow from one of their own number from which they will not for years recover.

But it must be remembered that Johannesburg is not the South African Republic, and that the bone and sinew of this republic is made up of sturdy, rough, God-fearing, unprogressive, Bible-loving, behind-the-times burghers; good stock, in spite of their unprogressive mediævalism, to found an empire upon. This element gives strength and stability to the little republic; this element it is which President Kruger understands so well and interprets so accurately. His burghers believe in his sturdy, rugged, God-fearing, if somewhat warped and twisted, character, and he trusts and builds his republic on his burghers.

These are the people, far off upon the remote farms and not in the crowded slums of Johannesburg, that England or any other power would have to reckon with in subduing the South African Republic.

These are the kind of people who largely make up the sister republic of the Orange Free State. Happily for the Free State Boers, gold has never been found in large paying quantities within their borders. They have, to be sure, a few diamond fields within their territory; but the centre of the diamond interest is still in Kimberley, within the limits of the Colony of the Cape of Good Hope.

The Orange Free State is one of those happy lands without a history—at least without a history tarnished with blood or stained by rapacity or greed. Its people, rough, vigorous, virile, though few in numbers, are strong in the primitive virtues of an unspoiled race. Its capital and largest city, Bloemfontein, is a village of five or six thousand inhabitants.

I had a pleasant call upon President Steyn, its chief executive, who struck me as a stalwart, honest, earnest man desirous of doing his best and utmost for his little republic. Unlike President Kruger, he is a man of education and refinement, and would grace any presidential chair.

I saw also the opening of the Raad, the legislative assembly of the Orange Free State. It is a congress of giants, a parliament of stalwarts. All of its twoscore members average, I am told, over six feet in height. They are broad in proportion and "bearded like the pard."

A most impressive sight it was to see these splendid specimens of physical vigor file in and take the oath of allegiance for their new term of service. Not a puny one among them; not a weakling or a human hothouse plant; a senate of farmers it is, with generations of sturdy Dutch blood in its veins. These are the representatives of the people that make South Africa a factor in the family of nations.

The English-speaking residents of South Africa are more progressive, more wide-awake, as a class more intelligent, but they have not made South Africa their own as have the Dutch Boers.

Said a wise and representative Dutch minister of Cape Colony to me:—

"South Africa is our home. We have never known any other. We do not want any other. Our supreme allegiance is not to Great Britain; least of all is it to Holland; it is to South Africa. Here, in the Cape, we are willing to live for the present under the dominion of Great Britain, but we do not believe it will last forever. We want to found a nation of our own. The English who come here are always thinking and talking of 'going home.' South Africa is not their home, and they never regard it as such. As soon as one of them makes a little money he hurries off to England to spend it. The thousands of emigrants who are always coming to the Cape come not to found a home, but to make all they can out of the country that they may spend it somewhere else. South Africa is owned by absentees. Even the poor people who will never scrape together shillings enough to pay for a steerage passage to Europe are nevertheless always talking about 'going home,' and the colored people with a little English blood in their veins, when they wish to put on airs talk about 'home.' With us Boers it is different. This is our home. We are Africanders. Here our fathers lived and our grandfathers. Here we were born and here we expect to die."

The English are superb colonizers. More than any other nation they make the solitary places joyful and the desert to blossom as the rose. No other race can approach them in colonizing and in governing ability. In India and Egypt, in Hong Kong and the Straits they have brought order out of chaos, and in Australia and New Zealand they have found and peopled new continents. This is their one amiable weakness as colonizers—they never get weaned, even in the third and fourth generation, from the old home. Admirable as is this power of Britain to claim the allegiance of all her children even though they wander to the antipodes, the very affection which they bear to the mother country carries with it this element of weakness when they are brought in contact with a homespun and a home-bred race like the Boers.

If a war should arise—which may Heaven forbid!—the Boers would be fighting for home and country, the English for domination and conquest. But war, in my opinion, at present is very unlikely. Great Britain is too powerful and President Kruger is too shrewd. The Dutch republics would have little to gain and much to lose by a war which might result in complete independence, but in all probability would result in making all South Africa a British colony.

For the present doubtless the *status quo* will be maintained, and the two little republics of Dutch farmers in central South Africa will complete the century as independent States under " the sphere of British influence."

But what changes the new century will bring to the map of South Africa, who can tell?

XXXIX

A CALL ON "OOM PAUL"

President Kruger at Home

SUCH an interesting personality has the President of the South African Republic that the story of an interesting call upon him is worth recording.

Was it ever seen since the world began that the eyes of the civilized nations were fixed on an old Dutch Boer in the heart of South Africa, an old man who can scarcely read or write, yet has the power by native wit and shrewdness, and a rare conjunction of circumstances, to dictate his own terms to the mightiest empire in the world, and perhaps to set by the ears the nations that represent the highest civilization in the world?

Yet this is the position held by that much bepraised and much bespattered man, President Kruger of the South African Republic.

Christian Endeavor meetings called me to Pretoria, the capital of his republic, for two days, and during those days I saw the old president three times. Since he will be a marked character in the history of the last two decades of the nineteenth century, whatever the outcome of the present troubles may be, the impressions left by these glimpses of the old Boer president are worth recording.

The first time I saw him he was returning from the outskirts of the town in his carriage, and the only impression I received was of royal display that scarcely comported with republican simplicity. Before him galloped half a dozen armed troopers, and behind him as many more bearing the colors of the republic, while out of the carriage-window beamed the face of an old man. A passing glance would lead one to think that he was the last man to hold the destiny of a considerable section of the earth's surface in his hands. If the president of the United States should put on such style as "Oom Paul" displays in his daily drives, he would be laughed at as a snob and an aristocrat; but then, the president of the Transvaal may claim, with some show of reason, that since the Jameson raid a body-guard is no mere ornamental appendage.

My next view of this historic old man was at closer quarters. He was going to his executive office in the Volksraad, or State House of the Transvaal. The inevitable troopers galloped before, grounded arms, and saluted as the old president alighted from his carriage, and made his way with bent back, but strong and sturdy steps, up the steps and along the passage to his office.

Should you meet him in Cabbagetown, England, or in Wayback, U. S. A., you would say: "There is a good, common-sense farmer. He is probably a deacon in the orthodox church; and, when work on the farm is slack, he is not above sitting on a cracker-box and discussing turnips with the other magnates of the village store."

But such a man must be judged at home. He does not shine on dress parade, or in circles where you expect pomp and circumstance and court etiquette, it must be confessed. In both the American and the English senses of the word, he is a "homely" man, and I was fortunate enough to have a chat with him under his own vine and fig-tree.

Armed with no letters of introduction, which in the circumstances would have been quite superfluous, I went under the convoy of Pastor Bosman, one of the worthy and learned Dutch Reformed ministers of Pretoria.

Imagine a low, one-story, gable-roofed cottage, embowered in trees and vines, and standing close to one of the principal streets of a rather straggling and unkempt village: and you will picture to yourself the abode of one of the most famous men of modern times. It looks like anything but the abode of royalty, or even of a high republican dignitary; and, if it were not for the two soldiers before the door, you would suppose that you were entering the home of one of earth's toilers; say an engineer on a railway or a country parson.

Before the door are the famous marble lions presented by Barney Barnato, the great South African speculator. From the artistic point of view they will not detain us long from the genuine lion of South Africa, who sits there in all democratic simplicity in a wicker chair upon his front porch, smoking a long briarwood pipe.

If President Kruger seems to put on rather an undue amount of royal style and dignity when on the street, it cannot be said that he carries it too far when he passes his own front gate. Nothing could be more simple or more primitively democratic. No cards are required, no liveried flunky receives you, no etiquette or formality bars the way. You simply walk past the guards, step up on the veranda, stretch out your hand, and say, "How do you do, Mr. President?" If you can say it in Dutch, so much the better, for President Kruger speaks no other tongue.

As you take his cordially outstretched hand, you see that he is by no means an impressive-looking man. An old man of fully threescore and fifteen, if we may judge by his looks, whatever the family Bible says, in a blue suit somewhat the worse for the wear, and an antiquated beaver hat,—in which he must do everything but sleep, for he always appears in it,—stands before you. Under his chin and around his capacious neck is a fringe of white whiskers, such as the irreverent small boy in America would call "galways." A stubby length of beard of four days' growth does not *adorn* his face, and his good-natured blue eyes twinkle over an undeniably bulbous nose.

My kind friend, Pastor Bosman, introduced me as "Dr. Clark, from America."

"Ah," said the president in Dutch, "are you one of those Americans who always run to the Queen when you get into trouble?"

To show me at the same time that he was not very serious, he turned around with a chuckle, and before I could answer him through my interpreter, gave me a hearty slap on the shoulder.

When Mr. Bosman told him of my life-work, and that my present visit to Pretoria was in connection with the Christian Endeavor movement, he replied: "Ah, that is good. I love all those who love the Lord Jesus Christ. When we love Christ, there is a link that binds us all together."

Then I told him that in America, too, we rejoiced in having a Christian president, that we had often been thus favored, and that ex-President Harrison's cabinet was even called in pleasantry "a Presbyterian cabinet," there were so many Presbyterian elders in it.

"I am glad you have such good rulers," said the old man; "for the nation that fears God and obeys him is the only prosperous nation."

Remembering that President Kruger was converted under the preaching of Mr. Lindley, one of the pioneer missionaries of the American Board to Africa, I told him that I belonged to the same church in America as did Mr. Lindley.

At this the old man's eyes glistened, for he loves and reverences the memory of his spiritual father; and he said with genuine warmth: "Ah, he was a good man, he was a good man. He preached Jesus Christ. We all need Christ's strength"; and again he repeated, "Those of us who love him, whatever our creed, should love one another."

A young Boer, unkempt and slouching, and evidently just from the back country, was waiting to see Oom (uncle) Paul, as all the Boers affectionately call the president of the Republic, and I did not trespass long upon his time.

With a cordial hand-shake he bade me goodby, and I went down the steps between Barney Barnato's marble lions, feeling that, however narrow and misguided the president of the

South African Republic may be in many matters of public policy, he is a sincere Christian, a Christian of the severe, Old Testament type, perhaps, but nevertheless a man who tries to do his duty.

XL

IN THE ORANGE FREE STATE

Look on the map of South Africa, my fellow travellers, and journey with me, if you will, from Bloemfontein across the border of the Orange Free State, over the beautifully diversified eastern district of this Cape Colony until we come to the seacoast of East London, and then inland again until we come to the old town of King William.

It seems like a mere thumb-nail distance on the map; a fly on a globe could step across it in three steps; yet on so large a scale are things built in this part of the world that it has taken me more than thirty-six hours continuous railway travelling to cover this distance.

The Christian Endeavor meetings in Bloemfontein, the capital of the Orange Free State, were well attended, and, I hope, of profit. There are only two societies in that little capital, one in the Dutch Reformed church, and one in the Baptist church; but there is good material for a round half-dozen if all the churches take up the work. Rarely have I found myself in a more delightful Christian home than in that of "his worship," Mayor Sowden of Bloemfontein.

As in many other towns in the Transvaal and the Free State, some of the Endeavorers here speak Dutch and some English.

One of the leading Dutch ministers in Johannesburg gave me this greeting, which I will pass on to you:—

> JOHANNESBURG ZENDT GROETEN,
> ONZE GOD ZEGENE U EN MAKE U
> TEN ZEGEN VOOR DE WERELD.

Dutch is so much like English that I need not translate this message, except to tell you that "zegene" is the verb "to bless," and "zegen," the noun "blessing."

In Johannesburg, too, at the close of one of our Endeavor meetings, we sung the doxology, as becomes an interdenominational and international society, in two languages, some singing in Dutch and some in English. Yet this is the city that some people do not consider it safe to visit in these days, from which come wars and rumors of wars between the Dutch and English.

Surely Christian Endeavor in such meetings may have this blessed privilege of bringing diverse and even hostile races together when both love the same Lord.

I did not have long to stay in this peaceful

RUNAWAY KRAAL GIRLS IN A MISSION SCHOOL

little republic, but hurried on to Cape Colony. Before crossing the border I had to be very thoroughly disinfected, lest I should bring with me the dreaded rinderpest, which has swept off the cattle of the Transvaal. First I was fumigated; then my boots were soaked in diluted carbolic acid, and my clothes were brushed off with the same; and then all my belongings, down to a trunk-strap and umbrella, were fumigated for half an hour; and after that I was allowed to cross the border. So you see that travelling in South Africa in this year of war and locusts and rinderpest has its peculiarities, to say the least.

Two very pleasant days I spent in East London in the Old Colony, *i. e.*, the Cape of Good Hope. How familiar "the Old Colony" sounds in Massachusetts ears!

East London, beautiful for situation, must be considered one of the Christian Endeavor centres in South Africa, since it has three societies, two Presbyterian and one Baptist, with a good prospect of two or three more Juniors before long. The meetings were well attended, and there was more genuine Christian Endeavor enthusiasm than I have always seen. But everywhere in this continent it is the day of very small things Christian Endeavor-wise, and the few here who are interested have to remind themselves, "God hath wrought large things through Christian Endeavor in other lands; why not in Africa?" Is South Africa an exception to every other land, and the only country to which Christian Endeavor is unfitted? I cannot believe it, and, though these are the days in many places, not even of seed-sowing, but of laborious sod-breaking, I believe the harvest will come.

XLI

HOW BISHOP TAYLOR READ THE BIBLE

A Memory of Family Worship At Lovedale, South Africa

As I have before said, one of the most interesting places in all South Africa is Lovedale, in the colony of the Cape of Good Hope. Far from a railway, it must be reached by a bone-racking, seven hours' jolt in a post-cart. But it is well worth the journey, were it ten times as long and hard; for here in the heart of South Africa is an institution which fulfils all one's ideals of what a Christian mission school should be, a school which does not forget that it is Christian because it is scholarly.

Substantial building, modern appliances, wide-awake teachers, and a constituency of pupils drawn from almost every part of Africa, make it attractive. Kaffirs, Fingoes, Bechuanas, Basutos, Zulus, West Coast Africans, dwellers in the Congo, and I do not know how many other tribes here send their boys, the picked youth of Africa. Most of them understand either Kaffir or Sesuto, as the language of the Basutos is called.

Of course Lovedale has its leading spirit, as every such place must have, some one whom

God has raised up to make it what it is. In this case, as every one in Africa will admit, it is Dr. James Stewart, of the Free Church Mission, who, more than a generation ago, came to Lovedale, here to embody his ideas of a Christian education.

"There are three great men in South Africa," said one of his enthusiastic admirers to me one day, "Sir Cecil Rhodes, President Paul Kruger, and Dr. James Stewart," and, if Dr. Stewart's fellow teachers and pupils could decide the matter, Dr. Stewart's name, like Abou Ben Adhem's, would lead all the rest.

But it is not altogether of Dr. Stewart that I would write in this article, but of still another remarkable man who has done much to make the Dark Continent brighter. I had been cordially invited by Dr. Stewart to speak to the hundreds of pupils of Lovedale concerning Christian Endeavor and its possibilities of service for the young, and at the same time to make his hospitable home my own. Whom should I find already domiciled as a guest in that home but the venerable Bishop William Taylor, the evangelist of four continents, whose name, however, will ever be indissolubly linked with the last continent to which he has given his manhood's strength and his declining days?

A most venerable figure is Bishop Taylor, with a long, gray beard sweeping a stalwart chest, a smile that is sweet and benignant, and a step that, when occasion requires, is still brisk and sprightly.

One of the most vivid scenes, photographed on my memory, of three memorable days at Lovedale, was of family prayers on the morning when Bishop Taylor was asked to lead.

There sat the venerable bishop with the big Bible open on his knee. Near by sat Dr. Stewart, the companion and friend of Livingstone and Moffat and Drummond and almost every other man who has come to shed light on darkest Africa. In other parts of the large room sat Mrs. Stewart and five of her seven charming daughters, the mother, if she will allow me to say so, looking almost as young and quite as charming as any of them. In a row together sat the four or five Kaffir servants of the establishment, representatives of the dark tribes to whom both Dr. Stewart and Bishop Taylor have devoted their lives.

The bishop is troubled with bronchitis, which has affected his voice not a little (only temporarily, let us hope), and he speaks, perhaps to save breath, in a peculiarly abrupt, not to say jerky, way, often omitting his pronouns and articles, and chopping off his racy sentences so that they shall contain no superfluous words. But this method only adds a new piquancy to his commentary, as with the strong common sense and picturesque imagery which made him so popular among the '49ers of California, the Spanish Americans of South America, and the gold-diggers of Australia as well as among the dwellers on the Congo and the Zambezi in later years, he opens up the Scriptures.

Literally "opens up." I have heard that phrase used many times, but I have seldom so fully understood its meaning. It was as if the good bishop pulled off cover after cover from caskets containing the jewels of God's word, and showed us the heaps of gems beneath. I can but very faintly reproduce that exposition; for you must be in Lovedale in the midst of the Stewart family, and hear the good bishop's tones, to understand it fully; but let me do as well as I can.

The passage he chose was the familiar one hundred and third Psalm.

"A man, one fine day, had a talk with himself," began the bishop in his abrupt way. "Had a conversation with himself. Here is what he said. 'Bless the Lord.' He counts up five benefits,—five things the Lord has given him: first, pardon, 'forgiveth all thine iniquities'; second, health, 'healeth all thy diseases'; third, redemption, 'redeemeth thy life'; fourth, mercies, 'crowneth thee with 'em'; fifth, satisfaction, 'satisfieth thy mouth' even; then of course thy soul. Gives thee youth in old age.

Just what we old men want. Youth like the eagle's, too, soaring, aspiring, glorious youth."

* * * * * *

Thus the exposition went on, something fresh, quaint, or piquant about each verse. The ninth verse is reached. "He will not always chide; neither will he keep his anger forever."

"'Look here, my soul,' David says, 'you need chiding.' The Lord knows he did, too! 'But God will not nag you. He will not scold, much as you deserve it. He treats you a great sight better than you deserve.' 'He hath not dealt with us after our sins.'

"And now he tells us how much God loves us. First, the perpendicular measurement, 'as the heaven is high above the earth'; second, the horizontal measurement, 'as far as the east is from the west'; third, the affectionate measurement, 'like as a father pitieth his children'; fourth, the measurement of tare and tret. He makes allowances. He knows how earthy and dusty we are. 'He remembereth that we are dust.'

"Then David reminds himself how little and frail he is. Grass. Flowers. The red poppy in the field. Swish goes the scythe. Where is it? Even if there is no scythe, a breath of wind comes, and the poppy is gone. So man's life. 'But, O soul,' says David, 'if your earthly life is short, your real life stretches between two everlastings. God's mercy is from everlasting to everlasting.' How far is it between two everlastings? When you can find out, you know how long your real life and how wide God's mercy is.

"No wonder it takes angels and ministers and all his works in all places to bless the Lord for such mercy. Ends as he begun. Beautiful frame all around picture. 'Bless the Lord, O my soul.'

"Let us pray."

After a fervent prayer we rose from our knees and went our several ways, the one to his classroom, another to his books, another to her housework, but all better fitted for our duties because of this refreshing morning draught at the fountain of God's mercy.

I will not promise that I have quoted accurately every word and turn of thought of the good bishop, for it was some weeks afterward, on the long voyage through tropic seas from Cape Town to Southampton, when I first had opportunity to write out my scanty notes. But I feel confident that in some measure I have caught the spirit of that hour of morning worship in Lovedale, and to a large extent have remembered the bishop's phrases, for his are winged arrows that stick. As they take flight once more in these columns, may they again find their mark.

XLII

THE WORLD'S GREAT DIAMOND VAULT

ONE of the most unique places on the earth is Kimberley, in South Africa. There is situated the world's great diamond vault. The exciting thing about the vault is the uncertainty of its contents. No one knows how deep it may be, or how many hundreds of millions' worth of diamonds it may contain. Its length and width, however, have been pretty accurately determined; and twenty-five years of careful prospecting have proved with some degree of certainty that no other such great vault exists in South Africa, and probably in no other part of the world. The diamonds of India and Brazil have paled their ineffectual fires before the *blink Klippe* (bright eyes) as the Dutch Boers call them, of Kimberley. It was in the year 1867 that the first "bright eye" was found on a table in Schalk Van Niekerk's farmhouse, in the Hopetown district of South Africa, south of the Orange River. The man who made the discovery bore the unromantic name of O'Reilly, proclaiming in his very patronymic that a son of the Emerald Isle had found a stone more precious than emeralds. I have said he found it on the farmhouse table, but the children of the house had previously found it in the dry river-bed, and had brought it with other "pretty stones" to the farm, when fortunate O'Reilly, trader and hunter, saw it. This find naturally set others to searching for *blink Klippes*, especially when it became known that a competent authority declared Mr. O'Reilly's stone worth $2,500 at the least. Here and there other "bright eyes" were found. Some children picked a few out of the mud wall of their father's house. The mud of which this wall was made naturally became an object of interest, and more diamonds were found in it. Thus in various ways interest and expectation were kept alive.

A native witch-finder proved to be a diamond-finder as well, for in his possession was discovered a pure brilliant of the first water, weighing eighty-three and one-half carats, and sold afterward to the Countess of Dudley for £25,000. For years the witch doctor had used the stone as a charm, and perhaps on this account the possession of the "Star of South Africa" is said to make the present owner more *charming* and *bewitching* than ever.

Of course there were not wanting those who "pooh-poohed" the whole idea of diamonds in Kimberley. One of these sapient individuals, a geologist, J. R. Gregory by name, advanced

the astounding theory that these diamonds
were brought in the crops of ostriches from
some far-off and unknown land. Moreover, he
proved beyond a peradventure, from the geo-
logical character of the district, "which he had
lately and very carefully examined," that it was
*impossible that diamonds had been or ever could
be found there.* And yet in about a year from
the publication of that absolutely convincing
statement, on this very ground the greatest
diamond mines which the world has ever known
were discovered—mines which yield every year
more than twenty million dollars' worth of diamonds. This brilliant geologist deserves to
rank with the equally brilliant scientific man
who demonstrated so conclusively that a ship
driven by steam could never cross the Atlantic
Ocean, whose treatise, as cruel fate would have
it, was carried across the ocean on the very
steamships which he demonstrated could not go.
But it is of more interest to know how the diamond fields look to-day. Imagine one of the
most dreary spots on the earth's surface, as it is
by nature, not as man has improved it; an immense, wind-swept table-land, more than four
thousand feet above the sea-level, parched in
summer and occasionally drowned out in winter,
an arid desert plain fit for cactus shrubs and
prickly-pears, and ostriches and goats that can
digest pebbles and thorn-bushes; a portion of

the earth's surface which thirty years ago the boldest prophet would never have ventured to predict could ever support a hundred white men! Here, to-day, you find a thriving city of thirty thousand people, stores and churches and schools, tennis-courts and football fields, cycle-tracks and clubhouses, and all the evidences, good, bad and indifferent, of modern civilization.

The first thing that attracts your attention as you roll into Kimberley on the rails of the very moderate and leisurely Cape Government railway, are the tall chimneys and shafts and "head-gear" for hoisting the "blue" diamondiferous soil from the vasty depths beneath. But such machinery, housed in ungainly buildings, is common to all mining camps, gold, silver, copper or diamond; and the first real peculiarity of Kimberley is the vast "floors" covered with a grayish blue soil, which stretch for miles along the railway line. These floors are fields, six miles in extent, on which have been dumped the diamondiferous ground. Forty thousand loads a week are laid down on these floors, each load averaging one carat of diamonds, worth almost seven dollars. That great field is a veritable Golconda. In that unpromising-looking dirt are tens of thousands of sparkling gems, worth millions of dollars—diamonds white and lustrous, diamonds yellow and orange, and perhaps pink, most rare and valuable of all; little diamonds and big diamonds, some of them worth a king's ransom.

Perhaps—who knows?—the biggest and most valuable gem the world has ever seen is glittering under that dull clod yonder. Then why not step over that wire fence which alone keeps you from the floors and help yourself? Not quite so fast, my friend! It is altogether improbable that you would find anything if you did step over into the floor; for diamonds, like some valuable and precious characters that I have known, keep very much out of sight. The diamonds are mostly imbedded in that hard soil which must lie for weeks in the open air before it can be pulverized and washed. A steam harrow, constantly running over it, hastens the process of disintegration; and it is a long, slow, tedious operation to get the jewels out; for—again to moralize for a moment—diamonds, like other things most precious, are not to be had for the asking.

Moreover, if you should attempt to step over that wire rope more than one pair of keen eyes would be upon you, and probably more than one threatening pistol-barrel would be levelled at your offending head. If by any chance you should find a diamond by the roadside, or should have one given you, the best thing you could do would be to throw it away, though it be the Kohinoor itself; for the one unpardonable sin in Kimberley is to have a rough diamond in your possession if you are not a licensed diamond-dealer. Murder, arson, burglary, assault, are all trivial crimes on the diamond fields compared with the one sin which has a whole set of initials all to itself—the sin of "I. D. B.," or, to speak less enigmatically, Illicit Diamond Buying.

So we will not step across the wire fence, but go on to that great building where the soil is washed and the gravel sorted. We produce the indispensable pass, the armed sentry lets us within the building, and now we are deafened by the din of machinery that takes the precious soil into its capacious cylinders, and disintegrates it, and shakes it about, and washes it, and then discharges the washed gravel diamonds and garnets into a very ingenious machine called the pulsator, where, by a constant throbbing, pulsating motion, the diamonds and heavy pebbles are shaken to the bottom, while the light stuff which contains no gems floats off on the top.

In the bottom of the pulsators are wire meshes of different diameters, which sort the pebbles into heaps of about the same size. But an untechnical writer need not try to describe complicated machinery to untechnical readers. Let us hasten on to the most interesting room of all. Here, on both sides of long tables, sit fifty men with heaps of the washed gravel before them. Who knows the untold wealth that may lie in those heaps of little wet stones? Each man has a steel knife of a peculiar shape and a tin box, not unlike a child's mite-box, with a slit in the top. With his knife he deftly spreads out the little stones on the table, with his quick eye sees the precious gems, which he picks out and drops into his mite-box.

The superintendent takes off the covers of some of the boxes and lets us look within. See, it is half full of diamonds, the result of the morning's work alone! Here is a man sorting larger gravel, and his tin box contains forty large diamonds! Another by his side is searching in a pile of medium-sized gravel, and he has more smaller ones, while still another has a heap of minute brilliants, not much larger than a pin-head, in his tin box. Again the gravel is sorted over by convicts, who cost the company only a shilling a day; and still more diamonds, overlooked in the first sorting, are rescued by them from the débris before it is cast out on the ever-accumulating mountain of "tailings."

Now, readers mine, set your guessing wits to work, and tell me how many dollars' worth of diamonds have been sorted this morning by the dozen white men and forty convicts behind the tables. Do you give it up? Then I will tell you. No less than sixty thousand dollars' worth! And this is the average find, year in and year out, from nature's inexhaustible vault at Kimberley. Since these mines were discovered sixty-five millions of carats, valued at four hundred and seventy-five millions of dollars, have been dug out and washed and sorted at these mines. As about five million carats go to a ton, nearly fifteen tons' weight of pure diamonds have been exported, and how many thousands of tons remain to be won no man is wise enough to say; for the bottom of the vault has not been sounded, and the deeper the diggings go the richer they are, as though in nature's great jewel box the best diamonds had settled to the bottom, like the plums in a pudding.

The largest diamond of South Africa, however, was not found at Kimberley, but at Jagersfonte, in the Orange Free State. This is said to be "the largest and most valuable diamond in the world." Its gross weight is nine hundred and sixty-nine and one-half carats, the color is blue-white, and the quality very fine. "Its value cannot possibly be estimated"; for it must be remembered that though diamonds of ordinary size have a recognized market value of from seven to one hundred dollars per carat, according to fineness, quality, color, etc., when the stone goes above one hundred carats its price is enormously enhanced with each additional carat. The length of this literally priceless jewel is about two and one-half inches, its greatest width about two inches, the extreme girth in width about five and three-eighth inches, and in length about six and three-fourth inches.

Two more places of great interest we must visit. One is the native compound, where the workmen are kept for three months at a time in a voluntary prison, not allowed to go out or in, or to communicate with their friends. Even the top of the great compound is covered with a wire netting, lest some workman throws out an innocent-looking potato studded with diamonds to a friend beyond the walls. When they are discharged from their three months' servitude they are searched and stripped and subjected to all sorts of nameless indignities, lest in their clothes or under their skin a brilliant be concealed. On one swarthy-skinned African a suspicious sore was once discovered. The doctor thought he ought to lance the wound, and there found three diamonds! The Kaffir had actually cut out a flap of skin, dug out the flesh of his leg and concealed therein the diamonds, putting the skin back in its place; but instead of healing, the wound had festered, and so discovered the living diamond mine.

Thousands of natives are often gathered in a single compound, and they come from all parts of Africa—Kaffirs, Basutos, Bechuanas, Fingoes and half a dozen other tribes. Most of them are "raw heathen," and no better opportunity for missionary work can be imagined than is here found. I am glad to say that many missionaries are taking advantage of it both here and in Johannesburg, and services are regularly held every Sunday, and frequently on week-days.

There are the men who blast and dig and hoist to daylight the blue ground. They stand at the beginning of the diamond industry, so to speak. At the other end, in the office of the De Beers Company, we find the finished product—the diamonds, sorted and sized and graded, waiting for shipment.

What a fairyland is this office! Diamonds galore! On every counter heaps of them! Little shining piles of white stones! A million dollars' worth awaiting shipment! A trusted official, employed in the office in examining and valuing the diamonds, shows us about. Here is a big one of two hundred carats, worth twenty dollars a carat. Here is a heap of ten-carat stones. Here is a twin stone; a clean cleft in the middle makes it "twins." A yellow stone is very valuable, but this deep orange is exceedingly rare and worth still more; while this little pink stone of only one fourth of a carat is of almost untold value, for only three or four pink diamonds have ever been found. These black spots render this heap of stones far less valuable, and their bad "faults" and scars make this pile fit only for drills or for polishing other diamonds. "How many of your diamonds are absolutely perfect?" "Only about eight per cent," replied our guide, as he carelessly ran his fingers through a hundred thousand dollars' worth of gems. How much like human nature! Some black spot, some off color, some flaw, some fault! Alas, how much smaller is the per cent of men and women than of diamonds that have no defect. "There's something spiles us all," said the old lady, when reflecting on her minister's irritability. Ah, yes; diamonds of the first water are always rare. But I need not linger on the ethics of diamond mining. The morals of the gem are many and obvious. Like the sorters at Kimberley, let each one pick them out for himself.

XLIII

UNTO THE THIRD AND FOURTH GENERATION

Some families seem to be chosen of God, as are some men, to accomplish a unique and notable work in the world. Such families are the Adams, the Harrisons, and the Beecher families of America, such are a half-dozen that might be mentioned in England, such pre-eminently is the Murray family of South Africa.

It is not often, indeed, that God honors a family by committing to it the evangelization of a continent, but it is scarcely too much to say that this is the high and unusual honor bestowed upon Andrew Murray the First, of Scotland, and his descendants.

I say Andrew Murray the First, for there is now Andrew Murray the Second, the most famous of the succession, whose devotional books are read every day in a multitude of homes; and Andrew the Third, who has devoted his life to the natives of Nyassaland. Several Andrews the Fourth are on the way, if I am not mistaken, though they are not yet out of knickerbockers.

Every part of South Africa has felt the influence of the Murray family from the Zambezi and beyond, to Table Bay. Every church calls them blessed; while the Dutch Reformed Church, the most influential of all throughout the continent, has been rejuvenated and actually transformed by their influence.

But to begin our story at the beginning with Andrew the First. Seventy-five years ago, as has been noted above, the Dutch Reformed Church of South Africa, becoming alarmed at the spread of rationalism and indifferentism in its midst, and, distrusting the clergymen that came from Holland, most of whom were avowed rationalists, sent to Scotland for some godly and learned young ministers who might break the Bread of Life unto the Boers in the great continent which they had chosen for their home.

Most fortunately for South Africa, one of those chosen for this great work of spiritual nation-building was a young man, Murray by name, no other than Andrew Murray the First. It had not been in the past annals a distinguished family as the world counts distinction. The father was a farmer, and the grandfather, and it was not a luxurious living that they wrung from the unwilling soil of Scotia. But, as God counts distinction, I think it must have been a famous family, for never was the promise to "the third and fourth generation" more literally fulfilled. One of the yeoman ancestors gave to his descendants this verse, which has been the covenant promise of the South African branch of the family:—

"As for me, this is my covenant with them, saith the Lord: My spirit that is upon thee, and my words which I have put in thy mouth, shall not depart out of thy mouth, nor out of the mouth of thy seed, nor out of the mouth of thy seed's seed, saith the Lord, from henceforth and forever."

"I was much surprised," said the Rev. Andrew Murray of Wellington, when visiting Canada a few years ago, "to find that another branch of the family who emigrated to the Dominion about the time my father came to Africa had a similar covenant verse for their own, though neither branch of the family had previously known anything about the other." Their covenant was recorded in Deut. 7:9:

"Know, therefore, that the Lord thy God, he is God, the faithful God, which keepeth covenant and mercy with them that love him and keep his commandments to a thousand generations." See how similar are the covenant verses, though the wide Atlantic and eighty degrees of latitude stretched between the two branches of this godly family.

Andrew Murray the First came to Cape Town about the year 1820, and was very soon assigned to the pastorate of the important church in Graaf Reinet, then as now one of the most important towns of Cape Colony. But before he started for his new pastorate, which then involved a serious journey of several weeks by horse or bullock-cart from Cape Town, a romantic event occurred, which was destined to have an incalculable influence upon the destinies of the Murray family of South Africa. This event was nothing else than a case of genuine love at first sight. The young dominie, while in church at Cape Town (whether in the pulpit or the pew deponent saith not) was struck by the fresh and lovely face of a young Dutch-speaking girl of Huguenot extraction. He made inquiries, found that she was as good as she was pretty, and (we pass over the easily supplied preliminaries) carried her off to the Graaf Reinet parsonage, his sixteen-year-old bride. Before she was seventeen she was the mother of John, afterward Professor John Murray of Stellenbosch, a revered and beloved professor of Theology, recently deceased. Then followed in rapid succession sixteen other children of whom I think twelve lived to grow up. The following is an incomplete list; Andrew the second, famous now the world around for his saintly life and writings; William, the greatly beloved pastor of Worcester, Cape Colony; Maria, the wife of Pastor Neethling of Stellenbosch, the university town of South Africa; Charles, honored as was his father whom he has succeeded in the pastorate of the beautiful church of Graaf Reinet; Jemima, now Mrs. Louw, the wife of a minister and mother of other ministers; Isabella (Mrs. Hoffmeyer), a name beyond most others revered in South Africa; James, a farmer brother whose health alone prevented him from studying for the ministry and who now has charge of the old homestead at Graaf Reinet; George, the pastor of another important church of Cape Colony; Helen, the efficient principal of a splendid school for young ladies at Graaf Reinet; and Eliza (another Mrs. Neethling), a widow, who with her accomplished daughters has opened another flourishing school.

Our space will not allow us to call the roll of the third generation. If we could do so, more than a hundred grandchildren would respond, many of whom are active and earnest ministers or missionaries or ministers' wives. Even the fourth generation already has not a few representatives, and all with their faces Zionwards. Each married child of Andrew the First has blessed the world on an average with about a dozen children, and some with more. Thus John has had sixteen, Andrew eleven, William twelve, Mrs. Neethling eleven, Charles fourteen, and George fifteen. I have never seen a more attractive photograph than the family group of Rev. George Murray and his wife and their fifteen hearty, stalwart, handsome boys and girls.

An example this for the puny, degenerate families of the present in Old England and New England alike, where a little brood of two are sometimes counted two too many.

But to return to the old Dutch parsonage of Graaf Reinet to which Andrew Murray the First brought his sixteen-year-old bride when the century was young. Never were children more fortunate in their mother than the numerous Murray children. Not that this is particularly to their credit, perhaps, but it was greatly to their advantage. Hers was one of those sweet, persuasive natures which mould and guide and bless without seeming to know it themselves, certainly without conscious effort. When asked how it was that her children had all turned out so well, she answered, "Oh, I don't know, *I* didn't do anything." But every one else knew, if she did not. *She just lived herself the life she wanted her boys and girls to live.* Her life was "hid with Christ in God," and they, through her, saw the beauty of holiness. Much of the mystic element which appears in the life and writings of her famous son was undoubtedly derived from his mother, who, while in the world, was not altogether of it. "Her chief characteristic," said one of her children to me, "was a happy contentment with her lot." She was always exactly where she wished to be, because she was where her Father in Heaven had placed her. She outlived her husband, Andrew Murray the First, by many years, and only a few years ago was laid in the grave by the hands of loving children and grandchildren. Many are the stories still extant concerning this sweet and tender little mother in Israel. One day one of her children found her helping her grandchildren in some charades they were playing, making masks and dressing themselves up in grotesque fashion. "Why, grandma," said this daughter in feigned surprise, "are you helping in such worldly things as charades? I'm shocked at you." "Yes, my dear," she replied, "I think the Lord Jesus would like me to make the children happy in this way." She was very fond of good stories, and would often sit up half the night when interested. She was somewhat ashamed of this weakness, as she considered it, and did not realize that it was but a natural craving of her sympathetic nature. But all her children realized that her wonderful serenity and gentleness and loveliness of character came not a little from the hours of long communion when she looked up into the face of the Invisible and thus learned to endure as seeing him.

If the Murray children were fortunate in their mother, they were scarcely less fortunate in their home. Imagine a beautiful oasis in a stony, forbidding desert, and you have a mental picture of Graaf Reinet where they were all born and brought up. The Karoo, as it is called, is a famous district of South Africa, arid, parched, streamless, the natural home of the ostrich and a hardy breed of sheep that live on the Karoo bush. It has, to be sure, a certain barren beauty all its own, a beauty which Olive Schreiner has best described. But Graaf Reinet does not need the pen of an Olive Schreiner to describe its beauty, for it is indeed the "Gem of the Karoo." A fertilizing stream runs through the town, making every street green with trees, and every garden to laugh with luxuriant bloom. Around it tower the curious, square-topped hills, typical of South Africa, and on every side is the desert. Perhaps the finest garden in Graaf Reinet is that of the old Dutch parsonage. In this parsonage all the Murray children were born, and in this garden they all grew up. In the garden are forty different kinds of grape-vines all loaded with luscious branches when I saw them. At one time, before the phylloxera did its deadly work, there were sixty varieties. One of these vines is fully three feet in girth, and is said to be the largest vine in South Africa, if not in the world.

So abundant is the fruit that a "Christian Endeavor grape social" is one of the distinguishing features of the Graaf Reinet social year. Once a year all the Christian Endeavorers of Graaf Reinet, at the invitation of Rev. Charles Murray, the present proprietor, turn themselves loose in the garden and eat their fill, but after the hungry boys and girls have gone Mr. Murray tells me you would scarcely know the fruit had been touched, so much is there of it. Besides grapes, you will find in this famous garden peaches, apricots, plums, and pears and cherries, tamarinds and loquats, pomegranates bursting their too full sides and displaying their ruby contents, date palms throwing down a shower of yellow fruit, almonds and walnuts, and I do not know how many other luscious fruits and nuts. "Help yourself," said my hospitable host, "there is no forbidden tree in all this garden." Besides the more useful trees are also found bamboo and cypress, glossy-leaved rubber trees as big as English oaks, Norfolk pines, and many another which at home we cultivate as rare exotics in our greenhouses.

Such was the garden of the Lord, for why should we hesitate to apply this title to the parsonage compound at Graaf Reinet, in which, as I have said, the Murray family grew up? "The chief characteristic of the household at Graaf Reinet was *reverence*," said Mrs. Neethling, the eldest daughter, who kindly gave me many of the facts of this article. "We all reverenced God and God's book and God's day.

The children reverenced their parents, and the servants reverenced their master and mistress. We reverenced God's day by keeping it strictly. The meat for the Sunday dinner was cooked on Saturday, the raisins for the 'yellow rice' (a kind of curry which is a favorite Sunday dish among the Boers) were stoned on Saturday. The grapes were picked and the house swept and the boots blacked the day before, and when Sunday came we all, down to the seventeenth little toddler, expected to go to church, all the older children three times a day, under the blistering summer sun (and it knows how to blister in Graaf Reinet), as well as when the cooler breezes blew."

And did this strictness and this churchgoing disgust the coming Murrays with religion? Let the stalwart, devoted lives of the dozen children that reached maturity and their hundred grandchildren answer this question and forever silence the namby-pamby religiosity that fears to expect too much of the children lest they be turned away from the church. It is not the Sabbath strictness but the unkindly and ungodly life of many a professed Puritan that has turned the children from the faith.

But the world is especially interested, perhaps, in one of the boys that grew up in the Graaf Reinet garden, Andrew Murray the Second. When he came to sufficient years, he was sent to Scotland for his education; graduated in the arts and then in theology, went to Holland a year or two to perfect himself in the Dutch language, and then returned to South Africa where his great life-work has been accomplished, and his many books have been written. He was a mere beardless boy when he first returned to Africa, only twenty years old and still more youthful in appearance. The rules of the church forbade his being ordained until he was twenty-two, so he was sent as a missionary to the Orange Free State and the Transvaal, a little parish about twice the size of England.

Still, it was large enough for a boy. And well did this beardless boy cultivate it. "Why, they have sent us a girl to preach to us," said one of the old Dutch farmers. But fragile as his appearance then was, there was no end to the endurance of this young preacher. He would go off for weeks at a time on horseback, holding services in some convenient centre on the Veldt to which, from scores and even hundreds of miles around, the Boers would come. A temporary church of reeds would be erected, backed and surrounded by hundreds of the big Dutch farm wagons. In this the boy preacher would discourse with all the fire and fervency and spiritual power which so live and breathe in his books.

"For six weeks at a time," on one occasion, "one hundred babies every Sunday were brought to me for baptism," he told me; "and in these rude reed churches I preached some of the sermons which the world has since asked me to put into books."

"I could shut my eyes, and it seemed as though an angel from heaven were preaching," said Mrs. Neethling, the sister, who for eighteen months kept house for him in Bloemfontein, when he was the pastor of the Orange Free State and the Transvaal.

It is very much the same with us, is it not, my reader, as we peruse his books which so throb with the spirit and power of God? We open our eyes to read, and it seems as if an angel from heaven were speaking to us out of the printed page. This is the plain unvarnished tale of one of the most remarkable and one of the most influential families which this generation or any other has known. Never was there a more remarkable fulfilment of the promise, "Instead of the fathers shall be the children." Never was the constancy of the covenant-keeping God more wonderfully demonstrated.

XLIV

LAST DAYS IN SOUTH AFRICA

The last week of my stay in South Africa was in some respects the most encouraging of all, and during these seven days the most important steps for the advancement of Christian Endeavor were taken.

I have not time to tell you of beautiful Worcester, which, like Zion, "stands with hills surrounded." There I was the happy guest of Rev. William Murray. It has an excellent school for girls under the care of two efficient American teachers, Miss Smith and Miss Lyman. Here, from all the assembled scholars, gathered in front of the principal buildings, I received a most flowery welcome.

I wish I could describe at length the delightful day at Wellington, the home of Rev. Andrew Murray, and the home as well, as you can easily believe, of one of the best Christian Endeavor societies in South Africa. What a greeting it was that you received, through your representative, my dear fellow-Endeavorers!

It was almost too much for a bashful man, until he remembered that he represented you, and then he held up his head, and marched bravely between two long rows composed of two hundred South African maidens, who were singing :

> " A welcome, a welcome, a welcome to thee ,
> A welcome to our sunny land, dear friend from o'er the sea ;
> Then welcome, thrice welcome, glad welcome to thee,
> We pray that all thy coming years may blessed be."

Fortunately he was supported in this walk by Miss Bliss, one of the American teachers of Wellington Seminary and one of the best friends Christian Endeavor ever had in Africa.

Let me tell those of you who do not know it that here in Wellington was established the first "South African Mount Holyoke." More than twenty-five years ago, at the invitation of Rev. Andrew Murray, two American teachers, Miss Ferguson and Miss Bliss, came out to establish a school for young ladies on the "Mary Lyon model." This school has been the mother of several others, in which scores of American teachers have been employed; and of all the good influences for the advancement of the Kingdom in South Africa, next to the church of God itself, these appeared to me the most hopeful.

A Keswick convention, under the leadership of Mr. Murray, was being held when I reached Wellington, and for one day it was turned into a Christian Endeavor meeting. It was a great joy to me to meet, and for a day to be under the guidance of one to whom, in common with tens of thousands of others, I owe so much spiritual life and light.

We must hurry on to Cape Town, the metropolis of South Africa, where *the* Endeavor Convention was held. But we did not leave Wellington altogether behind, for nearly a hundred delegates, under the lead of Miss Bliss, came to the meetings. Others came from Worcester, Stellenbosch, Graaf Reinet, and other places; and very pleasant and profitable meetings were held, though there were only one or two of us present who had ever been at an Endeavor convention before.

Necessarily, things were somewhat informal. Open parliaments, rallies, early prayer meetings, presentations of flags, Junior hours, etc., were conspicuous by their absence; and the voice of the American visitor was heard, I fear, too often. Nevertheless, the convention marked the beginning of better and larger days for Christian Endeavor in South Africa.

A most cordial welcome meeting was held on the last evening of April, in which many of the ministers of Cape Town of all denominations participated. May day saw three sessions of the convention,—morning, afternoon, and evening. Sunday had four services for me in three different churches, the closing one being in the Adderly Street Dutch Reformed church after the regular services were over. This is an immense church, the largest in Africa, and one of the largest in the world, seating three thousand people; and it was well filled.

My last night on South African soil was spent in Stellenbosch, a famous educational centre. Once more I found myself in the home of one of the Murray family, Mrs. Maria Neethling. Here, too, is a fine Christian Endeavor society, whose only difficulty is that it has so many active members that it is difficult for all to take part in an hour. Many lessons of trust and love and resignation were taught me in this last day in Mrs. Neethling's home, which, in some form, I hope to pass over to you one of these days.

Thus comes to an end this South African Christian Endeavor tour, for as I write I am speeding *homeward* (O how blessed an adverb after nearly ten months absence!) on one of the steamers of the Union line. In some respects, which I need not particularize, this has been one of the most difficult missions of my life. During these seven weeks in Africa I have journeyed for you (and with you in spirit) two thousand eight hundred miles, have made sixty-nine addresses for Christian Endeavor, and have visited almost every place of considerable size in Natal, the Transvaal, the Orange Free State, and Cape Colony.

Unite with me, my readers, in the prayer that this great continent, with its magnificent possibilities and glorious future, may be made the land of King Emmanuel, and that Christian Endeavor may have some worthy part in the coming victory.

Selections from

Fleming H. Revell Company's

Missionary Lists

New York: 158 Fifth Avenue
Chicago: 63 Washington Street
Toronto: 154 Yonge Street

MISSIONS, INDIA.

In the Tiger Jungle.
And Other Stories of Missionary Work among the Telugus. By Rev. JACOB CHAMBERLAIN, M.D., D.D., for 37 years a Missionary in India. Illustrated. 12mo, cloth, $1.00.

"If this is the kind of missionary who mans the foreign stations, they will never fail for lack of enterprise. . . . The book is withal a vivid and serious portrayal of the mission work, and as such leaves a deep impression on the reader."—*The Independent.*

The Child of the Ganges.
A Tale of the Judson Mission. By Prof. R. N. BARRETT, D.D. Illustrated. 12mo, cloth, $1.25.

Adoniram Judson.
By JULIA H. JOHNSTON. Missionary Annals Series. 12mo, paper, net, 15c.; flexible cloth, net, 30c.

Once Hindu, now Christian.
The Early Life of Baba Padmanji. An Autobiography, translated. Edited by J. MURRAY MITCHELL, M.A. 16mo, cloth, 75c.

William Carey.
The Shoemaker who became "the Father and Founder of Foreign Missions." By Rev. JOHN B. MYERS. Missionary Biography Series. Illustrated. *Twenty-second thousand.* 12mo, cloth, 75c.

William Carey.
By MARY E. FARWELL. Missionary Annals Series. 12mo, paper, net, 15c.; flexible cloth, net, 30c.

Alexander Duff.
By ELIZABETH B. VERMILYE. Missionary Annals Series. 12mo, paper, net, 15c.; flexible cloth, net, 30c.

Reginald Heber,
Bishop of Calcutta, Scholar and Evangelist. By ARTHUR MONTEFIORE. Missionary Biography Series. Illustrated. 12mo, cloth, 75c.

Heavenly Pearls Set in a Life.
A Record of Experiences and Labors in America, India, and Australia. By Mrs. LUCY D. OSBORN. Illustrated. 12mo, cloth, $1.50.

MISSIONS, PERSIA AND INDIA.

Persian Life and Customs.
With Incidents of Residence and Travel in the Land of the Lion and the Sun. By Rev. S. G. WILSON, M.A., for 15 years a missionary in Persia. With Map, and other Illustrations, and Index. *Second edition, reduced in price.* 8vo, cloth, $1.25.

Justin Perkins,
Pioneer Missionary to Persia. By his son, Rev. H. M. PERKINS. Missionary Annals Series. 12mo, paper, net, 15c.; flexible cloth, net, 30c.

Women and the Gospel in Persia.
By Rev. THOMAS LAURIE, D.D. Missionary Annals Series. 12mo, paper, net, 15c.; flexible cloth, net, 30c.

Henry Martyn, Saint and Scholar.
First Modern Missionary to the Mohammedans. 1781-1812. By GEORGE SMITH, author of "Life of William Carey," "The Conversion of India," etc. With Portrait, Map, and Illustrations. Large 8vo, cloth, gilt top, $3.00.

"This excellent biography, so accurately written, so full of interest and contagious enthusiasm, so well arranged, illustrated, and indexed, is worthy of the subject."—*The Critic.*

Henry Martyn.
His Life and Labors: Cambridge—India—Persia. By JESSE PAGE. Missionary Biography Series. Illustrated. *Eleventh thousand.* 12mo, cloth, 75c.

Henry Martyn.
Missionary to India and Persia. 1781-1812. Abridged from the Memoir by Mrs. SARAH J. RHEA. Missionary Annals Series. 12mo, paper, net, 15c.; flexible cloth, net, 30c.

The Conversion of India.
From Pantænus to the Present Time, A. D. 193-1893. By GEORGE SMITH, C.I.E., author of "Henry Martyn." Illustrated. 12mo, cloth, $1.50.

The Cross in the Land of the Trident.
By Rev. HARLAN P. BEACH, Educational Secretary of the Student Volunteer Movement. *5th thousand.* 12mo, paper, net, 25c.; cloth, 50c.

MISSIONS, AFRICA.

The Personal Life of David Livingstone.
Chiefly from his unpublished journals and correspondence in the possession of his family. By W. GARDEN BLAIKIE, D.D., LL.D. With Portrait and Map. *New, cheap edition.* 508 pages, 8vo, cloth, $1.50.

"There is throughout the narrative that glow of **interest which** is realized while events are comparatively recent, **with that also** which is still fresh and tender."—*The Standard.*

David Livingstone.
His Labors and His Legacy. By A. MONTEFIORE, F.R.G.S. Missionary Biography Series. Illustrated. 160 pages, 12mo, cloth, 75c.

David Livingstone.
By Mrs. J. H. WORCESTER, Jr., Missionary Annals Series. 12mo, paper, net, 15c.; flexible cloth, net, 30c.

Reality vs. Romance in South Central Africa.
Being an Account of a Journey across the African Continent, from Benguella on the West Coast to the mouth of the Zambesi. By JAMES JOHNSTON, M.D. With 51 full-page photogravure reproductions of photographs by the author, and a map. Royal 8vo, cloth, boxed, $4.00.

The Story of Uganda
And of the Victoria Nyanza Mission. By S. G. STOCK. Illustrated. 12mo, cloth, $1.25.

"To be commended as a good, brief, general survey of the Protestant missionary work in Uganda."—*The Literary World.*

Robert Moffat,
The Missionary Hero of Kuruman. By DAVID J. DEANE. Missionary Biography Series. Illustrated. *25th thousand.* 12mo, cloth, 75c.

Robert Moffat.
By M. L. WILDER. Missionary Annals Series. 12mo, paper, net, 15c.; flexible cloth, net, 30c.

The Congo for Christ.
The Story of the Congo Mission. By Rev. JOHN B. MYERS. Missionary Biography Series. Illustrated. *Tenth thousand.* 12mo, cloth, 75c.

On the Congo.
Edited from Notes and Conversations of Missionaries, by Mrs. H. GRATTAN GUINNESS. 12mo, paper, 50c.

MISSIONS, AFRICA.

Samuel Crowther, the Slave Boy
Who became Bishop of the Niger. By JESSE PAGE. Missionary Biography Series. Illustrated. *Eighteenth thousand.* 12mo, cloth, 75c.

"We cannot conceive of anything better calculated to inspire in the hearts of young people an enthusiasm for the cause."—*The Christian.*

Thomas Birch Freeman.
Missionary Pioneer to Ashanti, Dahomey and Egba. By JOHN MILUM, F.R.G.S. Missionary Biography Series. Illustrated. 12mo, cloth, 75c.

"Well written and well worth reading."—*The Faithful Witness.*

Seven Years in Sierra Leone.
The Story of the Missionary Work of Wm. A. B. Johnson. By Rev. ARTHUR T. PIERSON, D.D. 16mo, cloth, $1.00.

Johnson was a missionary of the Church Missionary Society in Regent's Town, Sierra Leone, Africa, from 1816 to 1823.

Among the Matabele.
By Rev. D. CARNEGIE, for ten years resident at Hope Fountain, twelve miles from Bulawayo. With portraits, maps and other illustrations. *Second edition.* 12mo, cloth, 60c.

Peril and Adventure in Central Africa.
Illustrated Letter to the Youngsters at Home. By BISHOP HAMMINGTON. Illustrated. 12mo, cloth, 50c.

Madagascar of To-Day.
A Sketch of the Island. With Chapters on its History and Prospects. By Rev. W. E. COUSINS, Missionary of the London Missionary Society since 1862. Map and Illustrations. 12mo, cloth, $1.00.

Madagascar.
Its Missionaries and Martyrs. By Rev. W. J. TOWNSEND, D.D. Missionary Biography Series. Illustrated. *Tenth thousand.* 12mo, cloth, 75c.

Madagascar.
By BELLE MCPHERSON CAMPBELL. Missionary Annals Series. 12mo, paper, net, 15c.; flexible cloth, net, 30c.

Madagascar.
Country, People, Missions. By Rev. JAMES SIBREE, F.R.G.S. Outline Missionary Series. 16mo, paper, 20c.

MISSIONS, CHINA.

Chinese Characteristics.
By Rev. ARTHUR H. SMITH, D.D., for 25 years a Missionary in China. With 16 full-page original Illustrations, and index. Sixth thousand. Popular edition. 8vo, cloth, $1.25.

"The best book on the Chinese people."—*The Examiner.*

A Cycle of Cathay;
Or, China, South and North. With personal reminiscences. By W. A. P. MARTIN, D.D., LL.D., President Emeritus of the Imperial Tungwen College, Peking. With 70 Illustrations from photographs and native drawings, a Map and an index. Second edition. 8vo, cloth decorated, $2.00.

"No student of Eastern affairs can afford to neglect this work, which will take its place with Dr. William's 'Middle Kingdom,' as an authoritative work on China."—*The Outlook.*

Glances at China.
By Rev. GILBERT REID, M.A., Founder of the Mission to the Higher Classes. Illustrated. 12mo, cloth, 80c.

Pictures of Southern China.
By Rev. JAMES MACGOWAN. With 80 Illustrations. 8vo, cloth, $4.20.

A Winter in North China.
By Rev. T. M. MORRIS. With an Introduction by Rev RICHARD GLOVER, D.D., and a Map. 12mo, cloth, $1.50.

John Livingston Nevius,
For Forty Years a Missionary in Shantung. By his wife, HELEN S. C. NEVIUS. With an Introduction by the Rev. W. A. P. MARTIN, D.D. Illustrated. 8vo, cloth, $2.00.

The Sister Martyrs of Ku Cheng.
Letters and a Memoir of ELEANOR and ELIZABETH SAUNDERS, Massacred August 1st, 1895. Illustrated. 12mo, cloth, $1.50.

China.
By Rev. J. T. GRACEY, D.D. Seventh edition, revised. 16mo, paper, 15c.

Protestant Missions in China.
By D. WILLARD LYON, a Secretary of the Student Volunteer Movement. 16mo, paper, 15c.

www.ingramcontent.com/pod-product-compliance
Lightning Source LLC
Chambersburg PA
CBHW031905220426
43663CB00006B/777